NEW DIRECTIONS FOR EVALUATION
A PUBLICATION OF THE AMERICAN EVALUATION ASSOCIATION

Gary T. Henry, *Georgia State University*
COEDITOR-IN-CHIEF

Jennifer C. Greene, *University of Illinois*
COEDITOR-IN-CHIEF

The Expanding Scope of Evaluation Use

Valerie J. Caracelli
U.S. General Accounting Office

Hallie Preskill
University of New Mexico
EDITORS

Number 88, Winter 2000

JOSSEY-BASS
San Francisco

THE EXPANDING SCOPE OF EVALUATION USE
Valerie J. Caracelli, Hallie Preskill (eds.)
New Directions for Evaluation, no. 88
Jennifer C. Greene, Gary T. Henry, Coeditors-in-Chief
Copyright ©2000 Jossey-Bass, a Wiley company.

Microfilm copies of issues and articles are available in 16mm and 35mm, as well as microfiche in 105mm, through University Microfilms Inc., 300 North Zeeb Road, Ann Arbor, MI 48106-1346.

New Directions for Evaluation is indexed in Contents Pages in Education, Higher Education Abstracts, and Sociological Abstracts.

ISSN 1097-6736   ISBN 0-7879-5433-0

NEW DIRECTIONS FOR EVALUATION is part of The Jossey-Bass Education Series and is published quarterly by Jossey-Bass Inc., Publishers, 350 Sansome Street, San Francisco, CA 94104-1342.

SUBSCRIPTIONS cost $65.00 for individuals and $118.00 for institutions, agencies, and libraries. Prices subject to change.

EDITORIAL CORRESPONDENCE should be addressed to the Editors-in-Chief, Jennifer C. Greene, Department of Educational Psychology, University of Illinois, 260E Education Building, 1310 South Sixth Street, Champaign, IL 61820, or Gary T. Henry, School of Policy Studies, Georgia State University, P.O. Box 4039, Atlanta, GA 30302-4039.

www.josseybass.com

NEW DIRECTIONS FOR EVALUATION

Sponsored by the American Evaluation Association

COEDITORS-IN-CHIEF

Jennifer C. Greene   University of Illinois
Gary T. Henry   Georgia State University

EDITORIAL ADVISORY BOARD

Benjamin Alvarez   Academy for Educational Development
Michael Bamberger   The World Bank
Donald Bezruki   Legislative Audit Bureau, Wisconsin
Len Bickman   Vanderbilt University
Deborah Bonnet   D. Bonnet & Associates
Roger Brooks   Legislative Audit Bureau, Minnesota
Jonathan Bruel   U.S. Office of Management and Budget
Valerie Caracelli   U.S. General Accounting Office
Eleanor Chelimsky   Consultant
Lois-ellin Datta   Datta Analysis
Terry Hedrick   Independent evaluator
Michael Hendricks   MH Associates
Ernest R. House   University of Colorado
Dionne J. Jones   Pacific Institute for Research and Evaluation
Lisa Klein   Kaufmann Foundation
Morris Lai   University of Hawaii, Manoa
Henry M. Levin   Stanford University
Richard J. Light   Harvard University
Mark W. Lipsey   Vanderbilt University
Melvin M. Mark   The Pennsylvania State University
Jules Marquart   Vanderbilt University
Sandra Mathison   State University of New York, Albany
Georg E. Matt   San Diego State University
Robin L. Miller   University of Chicago
Ricardo A. Millett   W. K. Kellogg Foundation
Mary Ann Millsap   Abt Associates
Michael Morris   University of New Haven
Michael Quinn Patton   Union Institute Graduate School
Ellen Pechman   Policy Studies Associates
Sharon Rallis   Harvard University
Eunice Rodriguez   Cornell University
Peter H. Rossi   University of Massachusetts
Robert St. Pierre   Abt Associates
Mary Ann Scheirer   Program Evaluation Consultant, Annandale, Virginia
Richard C. Sonnichsen   Management Consultant, Sand Point, Idaho
Charles L. Thomas   George Mason University
Edith P. Thomas   U.S. Department of Agriculture
Maria Defino Whitsett   Texas Education Agency
Joseph S. Wholey   U.S. Office of Management and Budget
Carl Wisler   Wisler Associates

AMERICAN EVALUATION ASSOCIATION, 505 HAZEL CIRCLE, MAGNOLIA, AR 71753

Editorial Policy and Procedures

New Directions for Evaluation, a quarterly sourcebook, is an official publication of the American Evaluation Association. The journal publishes empirical, methodological, and theoretical works on all aspects of evaluation. A reflective approach to evaluation is an essential strand to be woven through every volume. The editors encourage volumes that have one of three foci: (1) craft volumes that present approaches, methods, or techniques that can be applied in evaluation practice, such as the use of templates, case studies, or survey research; (2) professional issue volumes that present issues of import for the field of evaluation, such as utilization of evaluation or locus of evaluation capacity; (3) societal issue volumes that draw out the implications of intellectual, social, or cultural developments for the field of evaluation, such as the women's movement, communitarianism, or multiculturalism. A wide range of substantive domains is appropriate for *New Directions for Evaluation;* however, the domains must be of interest to a large audience within the field of evaluation. We encourage a diversity of perspectives and experiences within each volume, as well as creative bridges between evaluation and other sectors of our collective lives.

The editors do not consider or publish unsolicited single manuscripts. Each issue of the journal is devoted to a single topic, with contributions solicited, organized, reviewed, and edited by a guest editor. Issues may take any of several forms, such as a series of related chapters, a debate, or a long article followed by brief critical commentaries. In all cases, the proposals must follow a specific format, which can be obtained from the editor-in-chief. These proposals are sent to members of the editorial board and to relevant substantive experts for peer review. The process may result in acceptance, a recommendation to revise and resubmit, or rejection. However, the editors are committed to working constructively with potential guest editors to help them develop acceptable proposals.

Jennifer C. Greene, Coeditor-in-Chief
Department of Educational Psychology
University of Illinois
260E Education Building
1310 South Sixth Street
Champaign, IL 61820
email: jcgreene@uiuc.edu

Gary T. Henry, Coeditor-in-Chief
School of Policy Studies
Georgia State University
P.O. Box 4039
Atlanta, GA 30302-4039
e-mail: gthenry@gsu.edu

CONTENTS

EDITORS' NOTES

A knowledge base about evaluation use is an essential component of disciplinary knowledge in the field of evaluation (Shadish, Cook, and Leviton, 1991). The topic of evaluation use has been studied both theoretically and empirically over the last thirty years. Use is a multidimensional concept, and the various functions or types of use—instrumental, conceptual or enlightenment, and symbolic (or political or persuasive)—have become part of evaluation's lexicon. The importance of the topic is reflected in the *Program Evaluation Standards* (Joint Committee on Standards for Educational Evaluation, 1994), in which standards focused on utility are intended to ensure that an evaluation will serve the information needs of intended users. Over this past decade, the field of evaluation has substantially evolved and expanded. Shulha and Cousins (1997) note several trends in their review and synthesis of evaluation use literature—the importance of context, the diversification of the evaluator role, and the recognition that process use was a significant component of evaluation activity. The identification of process use, as articulated by Patton (1997), has further expanded the conceptual terrain of evaluation use. Weiss (1998) also suggests that we broaden the scope of evaluation use to consider other potential users, such as the program organization, client groups, and society as a whole. Other voices have contributed to the recent dialogue and have emphasized the need for advancing our understanding and knowledge about evaluation use (Chelimsky, 1998; Conner, 1998; Datta, 2000; Henry and Rog, 1998; Johnson, 1998).

This *New Directions for Evaluation* volume advances a reconceptualization of evaluation use that reflects the diversified and changing landscape of the evaluation discipline. Although some chapters are more heavily focused on theory and others on practice, each to some degree blends both. In this way, the volume represents a seedbed of ideas that can be discussed and researched over the next several years. Its focus is on theory and practice grounded in U.S. applications. The information in the volume is put forth in an hourglass fashion, beginning broadly with Kirkhart's advancement of a new theory of evaluation use, framed as evaluation influence. The volume progressively narrows its focus through the next three chapters on different aspects of evaluation use as learning (Preskill and Torres; Shulha; and Rossman and Rallis). Each of the three chapters is anchored in approaches to evaluation that highlight the evaluative process and learning from and about this process. Then in a case study of City Year (Brett, Hill-Mead and Wu), both process and results-based use become more clearly intertwined, and the full extent of evaluation influence is highlighted. In the last two chapters, the discussion about use is broadened once again. Henry's provocative critique considers the

1

potentially detrimental effects of elevating the importance of use, and Caracelli's closing commentary positions the discussion on reconceptualizing evaluation use historically and highlights the challenges at the outset of the new millennium.

More specifically, in Chapter One, Kirkhart reviews much of the literature that has led to our current thinking about use. She then puts forth a compelling argument for reconceptualizing evaluation use in terms of an integrated theory of influence. The theory incorporates three dimensions— source of influence, intention, and time frame. The resulting conceptual framework is inclusive of different paradigms and addresses both process use and results-based use, intended and unintended use, and episodic and instrumental use. The conceptual framework that is advanced is more encompassing than previous conceptions of evaluation use and serves an integrative function for the remaining chapters in the volume. Kirkhart concludes with reflections on the significance of a theory of influence for unresolved issues for further study.

Each of the remaining chapters links in one or more ways to aspects of Kirkhart's framework, which serves to elevate process use to the same status as results-based use. The next three chapters focus on process use and depict evaluation use as learning. Although learning from results is a part of these approaches, each approach begins with learning from and about the process of evaluation. The chapters are differentiated by their perspectives on (a) the overall rationale for thinking about evaluation influence and use as learning and (b) the concomitant ideas about the kinds of evaluation procedures, stances, and methods that can best fulfill the intended goal or rationale. Chapter Two by Preskill and Torres is noteworthy for its consideration of the process aspects of use as a mechanism for transformative learning in organizations. The authors position evaluation as a means for ongoing individual, team, and organizational learning in the workplace. The chapter elaborates on the role of the evaluator, which involves taking a clinical approach, boundary spanning, and using organizational diagnostic skills as a means for promoting transformative learning.

In Chapter Three, Shulha illuminates, by way of example, many of the concepts outlined by Preskill and Torres. The focus is on evaluative inquiry in organizations and the challenges that evaluators face when shifting to a learning framework. In today's information age, knowing how to use information is an essential ability for organizations, including schools. Shulha argues for evaluation as a process model, both to learn about something substantive and to learn about evaluative thinking or information use. She locates the process model within the context of a school-university partnership, that serves as a backdrop for discussing the challenges that evaluators face in conducting evaluative inquiry. Shulha describes a practical, participatory evaluation approach that highlights the evaluative process, through which all participants learn.

Rossman and Rallis, in Chapter Four, focus on learning as critical reflection and action toward improvement of the evaluand and its context. They also emphasize the learning potential of the evaluative process itself. The evaluator becomes a partner in knowledge construction. The importance of the critical inquiry process is underscored by the interactive processes that ultimately contribute to learning. The authors emphasize that when done right, "use as learning" becomes an integral part of the evaluation process, rather than something added later or even apart from it. They argue that processes of dialogue and critical reflection can best enable this view of evaluation use and influence.

In Chapter Five, Brett, Hill-Mead, and Wu discuss use at multiple levels by using a case example that links both to the organizational context outlined by Preskill and Torres and to the societal context addressed by Henry. In their examination of an evaluation of City Year, a national, multisite, not-for-profit organization, many of the theoretical ideas of the previous chapters are illustrated by practical application. The case describes a developmental process through its examination of both process and results-based use over time. It also illustrates the tracking of different patterns of influence at different system levels, as well as tracking use over time. The chapter exemplifies the power of intertwining both process and results-based use and well illustrates Kirkhart's framework of the overall influence of evaluation.

Chapter Six provides a dialectical counterpoint to the preceding chapters in the volume. Henry critiques and challenges the primacy of use as a focus of evaluation. He directs our attention instead to social betterment as the primary purpose of evaluation and cautions that a focus on use may shift resources toward administrative or organizational issues and away from social conditions and policy issues. Persuasive use, an ill-defined concept, is given extensive discussion. Henry presents persuasive use as important for achieving policy influence with evaluation findings but impossible to pursue directly in the design of evaluation studies.

In Chapter Seven, Caracelli uses a broad brush stroke to trace certain marker events that have influenced and are influencing the direction of evaluation. She summarizes and integrates the changing notions about use that have been highlighted by the previous authors and explores how their insights cut across disciplinary boundaries, contributing to our understanding about evaluation use today and providing a stimulus for further study.

Interest in evaluation use transcends paradigm differences and cuts across programmatic boundaries. *New Directions for Evaluation* has twice before devoted volumes to the study of utilization. Volume no. 39 (McLaughlin, Weber, Covert, and Ingle, 1988) focused on understanding this elusive construct and on identifying research and innovative practices that promote utilization. The shadow side of use, evaluation misuse, was examined in volume no. 64 (Stevens and Dial, 1994). The present volume provides more than an update of evaluative thinking on use. It is intended to advance a reconceptualization of use that elevates its importance and centrality in evaluation theory and practice.

Valerie J. Caracelli
Hallie Preskill
Editors

References

Chelimsky, E. "The Role of Experience in Formulating Theories of Evaluation Practice." *American Journal of Evaluation,* 1998, *19*(1), 35–55.

Conner, R. F. "Toward a Social Ecological View of Evaluation Use." *American Journal of Evaluation,* 1998, *19*(2), 237–241.

Datta, L-e. "Seriously Seeking Fairness: Strategies for Crafting Non-Partisan Evaluations in a Partisan World." *American Journal of Evaluation,* 2000, *21*(1), 1–14.

Henry, G. T., and Rog, D. J. "A Realist Theory and Analysis of Utilization." In G. T. Henry, G. Julnes, and M. M. Mark (eds.), *Realist Evaluation: An Emerging Theory in Support of Practice.* New Directions for Evaluation, no. 78. San Francisco: Jossey-Bass, 1998.

Johnson, R. B. "Toward a Theoretical Model of Evaluation Utilization." *Evaluation and Program Planning,* 1998, *21*(1), 93–110.

Joint Committee on Standards for Educational Evaluation. *The Program Evaluation Standards: How to Assess Evaluations of Educational Programs.* (2nd ed.) Thousand Oaks, Calif.: Sage, 1994.

McLaughlin, J. A., Weber, L. J., Covert, R. W., and Ingle, R. B. (eds.). *Evaluation Utilization.* New Directions for Program Evaluation, no. 39. San Francisco: Jossey-Bass, 1988.

Patton, M. Q. *Utilization-Focused Evaluation: The New Century Text.* (3rd ed.) Thousand Oaks, Calif.: Sage, 1997.

Shadish, W. R., Jr., Cook, T. D., and Leviton, L. C. *Foundations of Program Evaluation: Theories of Practice.* Thousand Oaks, Calif.: Sage, 1991.

Shulha, L. M., and Cousins, J. B. "Evaluation Use: Theory, Research, and Practice Since 1986." *Evaluation Practice,* 1997, *18*(3), 195–208.

Stevens, C. J., and Dial, M. (eds.). *Preventing the Misuse of Evaluation.* New Directions for Program Evaluation, no. 64. San Francisco: Jossey-Bass, 1994.

Weiss, C. H. "Have We Learned Anything New About the Use of Evaluation?" *American Journal of Evaluation,* 1998, *19*(1), 21–33.

VALERIE J. CARACELLI *is senior social science analyst in the Center for Evaluation Methods and Issues at the U.S. General Accounting Office. She serves as chair for the Topical Interest Group on Evaluation Use.*

HALLIE PRESKILL *is professor of organizational learning and instructional technologies in the College of Education at the University of New Mexico, Albuquerque. Her research and consulting work focus on developing evaluation learning communities.*

1

This chapter recasts evaluation use in terms of influence and proposes an integrated theory that conceptualizes evaluation influence in three dimensions—source, intention, and time.

Reconceptualizing Evaluation Use: An Integrated Theory of Influence

Karen E. Kirkhart

Use of evaluation has been a concern since the earliest days of the profession. Although some challenge the centrality of use in the identity of the profession (see Henry, this volume; Mushkin, 1973; Scriven, 1991), the primacy of use as a focus of evaluation is well recognized. It has bounded theories of evaluation, marked debates, and framed meta-evaluation inquiry. Historically, the evolution of evaluation use has been marked by an increasing recognition of its multiple attributes (Cousins and Leithwood, 1986; Johnson, 1998; Leviton and Hughes, 1981; Preskill and Caracelli, 1997; Shulha and Cousins, 1997). Nevertheless an inclusive understanding of the influence of evaluation has been hampered by the scope and language of past approaches. This chapter argues that it is time to step back and reconceptualize the terrain of evaluation's influence by mapping influence along three dimensions—source, intention, and time. Each of these is defined, justified, and illustrated in the sections that follow, acknowledging historical antecedents. The chapter highlights related issues raised by the three-dimensional conceptualization and closes with reflections on the potential utility of an integrated theory of influence.

Historical Context

Evaluators have shown a long-standing interest in the nature and extent of their work's impact. Historically, conversations about influence have occurred under several themes—internal and external evaluation, evaluator roles, evaluation as a profession, ethics and values, and use of results (Anderson and Ball, 1978; Suchman, 1967). As the profession grew, these

Figure 1.1. Expanded Understanding of Evaluation Use

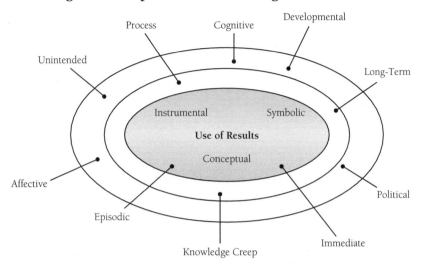

conversations became disconnected and our understanding of influence fragmented. The terms *utilization* and *use* were associated with the data-based influence of evaluation findings. When the narrowness of this perspective was recognized, the initial response was to bring other forms of influence under the umbrella of use; for example, the term *use* was attached to the influence of the evaluation process on persons and systems being evaluated *(process use)*. However, this has proven to be only a partial solution, one that in some ways has perpetuated the construct underrepresentation that it was intended to correct (Messick, 1995).

First, the term *use* is an awkward, inadequate, and imprecise fit with non-results-based applications, the production of unintended effects, and the gradual emergence of impact over time. Second, when the history of influence is traced from the perspective of results-based use, the historical roots of other dimensions of evaluation impact are erased. Process use, for example, incorrectly appears as an afterthought, a late arrival. Third, fitting other types of influence under a results-based paradigm continues to privilege the concept of results-based use. Other types of use are secondary, "tacked on," or seen as important primarily in the service of results-based use. This chapter argues that one cannot clearly perceive the influence of evaluation through a lens that holds results-based influence at its center, even though the lens may be expanded to include additional viewpoints (see Figure 1.1). A clearer vision requires a reconceptualization in which influence can be examined from multiple vantage points (this chapter identifies three), a framework in which previous understandings of results-based use can be repositioned and examined in a broader context.

As the citations in the following sections reflect, the various pieces of this model have been recognized and discussed before with varying degrees of emphasis, clarity, and detail. What is new here, however, is the integration of these pieces into a model that unites prior discussions. An integrated theory stands to move the field ahead insofar as it bridges previously fragmented conversations.

Importance of Language

The language of evaluation is itself an important topic of inquiry and reflection (Hopson, 2000). As Patton (2000) summarizes, "The evaluation language we choose and use, consciously or unconsciously, necessarily and inherently shapes perceptions, defines 'reality,' and affects mutual understanding" (p. 15). He further notes that a full analysis of an issue such as evaluation use necessarily leads us to consider the words and concepts that undergird our understandings and actions. The language shift proposed in this chapter is intended to broaden conversations and deepen communication.

This is not the first time that the field has questioned the symbolism of language and sought more accurate terminology in discussing the impact of evaluation. Weiss sought to align symbolic meaning with construct representation in suggesting a linguistic shift from *utilization* to *use*. In 1980, she noted the diffuse ways in which research knowledge affects policy, commenting, "Its influence is exercised in more subtle ways than the word 'utilization'—with its overtone of tools and implements—can capture" (p. 381). Her 1981 chapter went further. In it, she suggested that the term *utilization* embodies an inappropriate imagery of instrumental and episodic application and should therefore be abandoned. I strongly share her concern for selecting an accurate term that does not inappropriately constrict our understanding of the impact of evaluation; however, I disagree that the term *use* is a significant improvement over utilization. Not only are both terms instrumental and episodic, but they also imply purposeful, unidirectional influence. This chapter argues that in order to examine the question, How and to what extent does evaluation shape, affect, support, and change persons and systems? one must step back from a narrow construal of use and rejoin earlier broad-based conversations. A broader construct than use alone is needed to represent this integration—one that does not privilege results-based use over influence stemming from the evaluation enterprise itself, one that does not chronologically limit our vision of the effects of evaluation, one that looks beyond the sight line of our intentions. Toward this end, this chapter purposely shifts terminology—from use to influence—in proposing an integrated theory. The term *influence* (the capacity or power of persons or things to produce effects on others by intangible or indirect means) is broader than use, creating a framework with which to examine effects that are multidirectional, incremental, unintentional, and noninstrumental, alongside those that are unidirectional, episodic, intended, and instrumental (which are well represented by the term *use*). If we are truly interested in the effects of

Figure 1.2. Integrated Theory of Influence

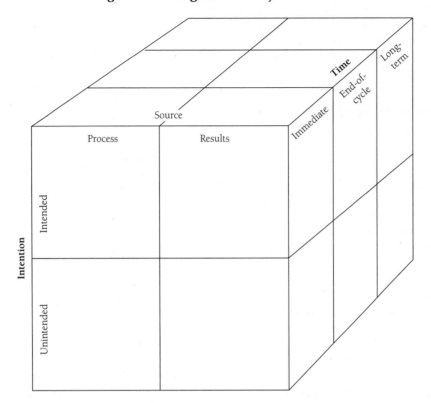

evaluation beyond the impact of the findings of the study, we need a conceptual framework that helps us see both the intended, immediate, results-based use (see the upper right-hand front segment of Figure 1.2) and other possible effects in the same picture.

An Integrated Theory of Influence

An integrated theory of influence incorporates three dimensions—source of influence, intention, and time frame.[1] Each dimension is subdivided into levels (see Figure 1.2). These subdivisions are admittedly somewhat arbitrary. Source, intention, and time may be more accurately characterized as continua, reflecting gray areas that fall between the levels. *Source of influence* refers to the active agent of change or the starting point of a generative process of change (Henry and Rog, 1998). Two levels address influences associated with the evaluation process plus influences associated with the results of evaluation. *Intention* refers to the extent to which there is purposeful direction to exert a particular kind of influence through the evaluation process or findings. It reflects the importance of considering both the intended and unintended influence of evaluation. The division of the third dimension, *time,* into immediate, end-of-cycle, and long-term influence reflects the need to recognize influence during and immediately following the evaluation cycle as well as effects that are visible in the future. These three dimensions and their historical antecedents are summarized in the following sections.

Source of Influence. The first dimension addresses the evaluation referent that is presumed to exert power or influence on individuals, organizations, or broader decision-making communities. Historically, the influence of evaluation was framed in terms of the use of results (Johnson, 1998; Shulha and Cousins, 1997). There was a parallel literature that concerned itself with the interpersonal influence of the evaluation process, but these two streams were not joined until the "discovery" of process use (Patton, 1998). Process use first emerged as a means of facilitating results-based use and then came full circle to be treated as a source of influence in its own right. However, remnants of this evolution that remain, reflected in the language of use, create conceptual problems. Process use is often erroneously tacked on to the recognized typology of results-based use rather than being viewed as an alternate typology in its own right. The linguistic shift from *use* to *influence* creates a framework for parallel treatment of the two dimensions, reflected in this model.

Results-Based Influence. Early attention to use of evaluation stemmed from a desire to maximize the positive social impact of evaluation, coupled with concerns over the perceived nonutilization of evaluation results (Ciarlo, 1981). Whether use was examined from the perspective of the policy-shaping community (Cronbach, 1982; Cronbach and Associates, 1980), the individual users, the decisions made, the organization being evaluated, or the reports issued (Weiss, 1981), the focal points of reference were the information produced by an evaluation and the data-based conclusions drawn. Cousins and Leithwood (1986) preface their review of empirical research on evaluation utilization with a definition of evaluation results as "any information associated with the outcome of the evaluation; for example, data, interpretations, recommendations; such information could be communicated at the completion of the evaluation or as the evaluation was proceeding" (p. 332). Although this definition clearly sets the stage for either formative or summative results-based use, early empirical emphasis was on summative use. Results-based use was first viewed in terms of instrumental use—direct, visible action taken based on evaluation findings (Rich, 1977). This narrow conceptualization quickly broadened to include conceptual uses of results, such as enlightenment and demystification, which captured cognitive impact on appreciations or understandings that did not necessarily lead directly to change in overt behavior (Rich, 1977; Weiss and Bucuvalas, 1980). A third type of results-based use addressed the role of evaluation findings in advocacy, argument, and political debate

(Greene, 1988a; Knorr, 1977; Leviton and Hughes, 1981; McClintock and Colosi, 1998; Owen, 1992, cited in Johnson, 1998; Shadish, Cook, and Leviton, 1991). Variously labeled legitimative use, symbolic use, political use, and persuasive use, this application explicitly focused on using evaluative information to convince others to support a position or to defend from attack a position already taken. Together these three vectors of use have delimited the conceptual landscape of results-based influence.

Process-Based Influence. Not all of evaluation's influence emanates from the formative or summative reporting of results. Sometimes the primary influence centers around the process of conducting the evaluation itself. Though the term *process use* did not appear in evaluation literature until the late 1980s, attention to the impact of the evaluation process can be traced to early literature on the change agent roles of the evaluator, to action research, and to models such as transactional evaluation, which emphasized the interactions between evaluators and open systems (Anderson and Ball, 1978; Argyris, Putnam, and Smith, 1985; Caro, 1980; Rippey, 1973; Rodman and Kolodny, 1972; Tornatzky, 1979). The roots and evolution of process-based influence are particularly visible in the history of participatory evaluation models (Brisolara, 1998).

Process use first emerged in the utilization literature as a means of facilitating results-based use. Greene's focus (1988b), for example, was on creating conditions conducive to results-based utilization, rather than on the intrinsic effects of the evaluation process itself. Subsequent treatments of process use emphasized its value independent of results-based use (Whitmore, 1991). Patton (1997) characterizes process uses as "ways in which being engaged in the processes of evaluation can be useful *quite apart from the findings* that may emerge from those processes" (p. 88, emphasis added).

Greene (1988b) posits three dimensions of process-based influence—cognitive, affective, and political. The cognitive dimension of process use refers to changes in understandings stimulated by the discussion, reflection, and problem analysis embedded in the evaluation process. Although process use may involve an instrumental component (as when reflection leads to a decision or action), the cognitive dimension focuses on enhanced understandings of the program among participants in the evaluation process. The affective dimension is more personally connected to the participants themselves. This dimension addresses the individual and collective feelings of worth and value that result from the evaluation process. Although Greene (1988b)construes affect as having psychological connotations of self-worth, other interpretations of affect are also possible (for example, feelings about evaluation, feelings about the program itself). The political dimension addresses the use of the evaluation process itself to create new dialogues, draw attention to social problems, or influence the dynamics of power and privilege embedded in or surrounding the evaluand. Recent models that position evaluation as an explicit intervention to modify program operations or to support program outcomes underscore the significance of the political dimension of process influence (Fetterman, 1994; Patton, 1998). These three types of process-based influence may work together. Shulha's discussion (this volume) of what evaluators themselves learned from participating in evaluative inquiry contains cognitive, affective, and political overtones.

Summary. The first dimension of an integrated theory of influence, source of influence, directs attention to the element of evaluation that is presumed to generate change. Broadly defined, these two sources of influence are the process of evaluation and the results that are generated. Particular models of evaluation may well respect both types of influence; however, many models give differential emphasis to the two sources of influence, and some focus almost exclusively on one source. Although typologies of use have developed within each source of influence, these distinctions should not overshadow the connections between process-based influence and results-based influence. Not only may the two types of influence be combined in a single logic model (see, for example, Greene, 1988b), but the subcategories within each source may be interrelated. Anderson, Ciarlo, and Brodie (1981), for example, discuss the affective dimensions of results-based use, whereas Greene (1988b) alludes to the instrumental impact of process use. In this volume, the structure of Henry's argument illustrates an implicit bridge between results-based and process-based use. The main focus of his chapter is results-based influence, but interestingly the crux of his argument for agenda setting—that evaluations can be useful in raising an issue—necessarily occurs during process use.

Intention. Intention is the second dimension of an integrated theory of evaluation influence (Kirkhart, 1999). Intention refers to the extent to which evaluation influence is purposefully directed, consciously recognized, and planfully anticipated. Most visible are the intended influences that are explicit in the purpose of the evaluation, in the theory employed, and in the evaluator-client contract. Latent purposes and covert evaluation agendas may also reflect intent, but these intentions may be more difficult to identify. Unintended influences capture the unforeseen impacts of evaluation on individuals and systems, often through unexpected pathways. Any given evaluation may have intended influence only, unintended influence only, or a mix of the two. Mapping both intended and unintended influences is essential to a full appreciation of evaluation impact.

The intent to influence (variously termed *intention* and *intentionality*) has figured significantly in the conceptualization of evaluation use. It is one of the early dimensions identified in building an integrated theory of influence (Kirkhart, 1995). Under other theories of use, it marks the boundary between use and misuse of evaluation (Alkin, 1990; Alkin, Daillak, and White, 1979; Christie and Alkin, 1999). The question that defines this second dimension of influence is, What are the intentions of the evaluator, client, and other key stakeholders concerning the influence of evaluation? Intention may be further deconstructed into three aspects—the type of influence that is desired or anticipated; who is to be influenced; and the persons, processes, and findings that are expected to exert influence. Though the first two are often collapsed, separate reflection facilitates identification of unintended influences.

Intended Influence. Evaluation may be purposefully directed to exert influence through either the process itself or the results produced. Patton's (1997) notion of primary utilization, *intended use by intended users,* marks a direct path between intention and influence. Historically, the most commonly envisioned scenario is results based: potential users of evaluation information are identified early in the evaluation process, and their information needs shape the evaluation, from the questions posed to the data collected to the ways in which findings are communicated, maximizing results-based use. However, there may be a similarly explicit intention to influence organizations and social systems via the evaluation process itself, as illustrated by participatory evaluation. Cousins and Whitmore (1998) differentiate two streams of process-based influence in participatory evaluation, each with its own ideology and intention. In transformative participatory evaluation (T-PE), the intent is empowerment, social action, and change, whereas practical participatory evaluation (P-PE) intends to support program or organizational problem solving. Similarly, Patton (1998) describes "evaluation as an intentional intervention in support of program outcomes"(p. 229), which is a kind of process use, conceptualizing the natural reactivity of the data collection process as an intervention that reinforces what the program is trying to do.

An important caveat concerning intended influence is that not all intentions are explicitly communicated or otherwise made visible. The stated purposes of an evaluation represent manifest, overt functions; for example, a formative evaluation may be undertaken with the intent of improving the evaluand, whereas a summative evaluation may be undertaken to help a sponsor better allocate funds. However, intended influences could also include latent, covert evaluation functions (Scriven, 1991). For example, an evaluation with the manifest function of improving program effectiveness could also have a latent function of increasing program visibility in the community. An evaluation with a manifest function of demonstrating accountability and efficiency to sponsors could have reallocation of funds and downsizing as latent intents. Capturing the full range of intended influence requires attention to both manifest and latent functions. Here the plurality of intended uses and users becomes critical. One must consider the understandings and agendas of the clients of the evaluation, the evaluators, and stakeholder audiences.

Unintended Influence. Evaluation may influence programs and systems in ways unanticipated, through paths unforeseen. Attention to the unintended influence of evaluation acknowledges both the power of ripple effects and our inability to anticipate all ramifications of our work. In evaluation, as in the programs themselves, unintended influence may be more impactful than intended influence. Moreover the territory defined by unintended influence is broader. Whereas primary utilization directs attention rather narrowly to intended uses and users, unintended influence is represented by a number of permutations. Three variations illustrate this point. First, intended users may exert influence in unintended ways or affect persons or systems other than intended. Consider a results-based example. An advisory panel is an intended user of the evaluation findings. Though their intended use was to make changes internal to the program, the data had unexpected policy implications that led them to initiate a community coalition to advocate for legislative change. This broader influence was unintended, though it was initiated by intended users. Second, unintended users may be involved in exerting influence, though the nature of the influence and the persons and systems affected are intended. Consider a process-based example in which a needs assessment is conducted on the problem of violence in public schools. The intention was to involve parents and teachers with school board members in identifying concerns and suggesting solutions toward a safe school environment; however, students asserted their interest in the evaluation, and their participation in the needs assessment altered the climate of the school. The influence was in the intended direction (toward safety) and on the intended system, but it came via an unintended user pathway. Third, the users, the nature of the influence, and the systems influenced may all be unintended. Consider an internal evaluation of a local human service agency intended to support a request for continued funding from its current community-based sponsor. As the evaluation unfolded, consumers played an unexpected role in the process, generating unintended positive publicity for the agency. The inclusive evaluation process was cited as a model, and a statewide consumer advocate group challenged public sponsors to rethink the parameters of the evaluation that they required for funding. Note that this unintended influence may be in addition to the intended use of the data to support continued community-based funding.

Summary. Intention is the second key dimension of an integrated theory of evaluation influence. Intended influences may be results based or process based, manifest or latent. Unintended influences may also link to process or outcome; however, the nature of influence, the persons or systems influenced, and the persons exerting the influence are other than desired or anticipated. Intended and unintended influences may occur singly or in combination, and as the examples cited previously suggest, they may be operative at different points in time. Though the examples offered illustrate positive influences, intention does not restrict the valence of the influence. Clearly, evaluation may have unintended negative influences on persons or systems, and even some of the intended influences may have negative implications for parts of the system. Taken together, the three dimensions of influence offer a framework within which to examine both the positive and negative impacts of evaluation.

Time. The third dimension, time, refers to the chronological or developmental periods in which evaluation influence emerges, exists, or continues.[2] This dimension highlights the dynamic nature of influence and the possibility of different dimensions of influence occurring at different points in time—immediate, end-of-cycle, and long-term. Because time is a continuum, this subdivision into three periods is arbitrary, but the categories draw attention to influence at three different stages that parallel the view of program outcomes as immediate, end-of-treatment, and long-term (Scriven, 1991). Just as those distinctions have been useful in directing evaluators' attention to program outcomes, a similar convention can guide the conceptualization of evaluation's influence.

Like the previous two dimensions, there are antecedents to the current treatment of time in the evaluation literature. Shadish, Cook, and Leviton (1991) characterize the history of use as moving from short-term to recognizing long-term use. This dichotomy was commonly used to describe the time dimension. Weiss (1981) included *how immediate is the use* (immediate versus long-term use) as one of six key dimensions in the conceptualization of use. Similarly, Smith (1988) included *immediate versus long-term* as one of four dimensions of use, although her analogy likening evaluation use to checking out books from a library is exclusively grounded in results-based use. Not all authors have treated time as a short versus long dichotomy. Wollenberg (1986, cited in Johnson, 1998), in a study of use that spanned a complete school year, conceptualized the time dimension as three periods or cycles of program implementation or growth—conceptual stage, developmental stage, and institutional stage. Cronbach (1982) outlined four periods of influence, noting, "An evaluation feeds social thought as it is planned, as it brings in data, as it comes to a close, and, one may hope, for several years thereafter" (p. 318).

Historically, the three dimensions of an integrated theory of influence—source, intention, and time—have intertwined. The time dimension has been attached to other use distinctions in ways that have blurred the full range of chronological influences. Leviton and Hughes's review (1981) illustrates how the time dimension was frequently folded into early discussions of instrumental versus conceptual results-based use. They cite Rein and White (1975) to mark early recognition of the fact that "problems in government are defined gradually over time, and decisions are eventually reached on the basis of an integrated set of information from many sources" (Leviton and Hughes, 1981, p. 531). The fact that this quotation is cited to illustrate instrumental versus conceptual use illustrates the historical confounding of dimensions—in this case, time with source. Similarly, in their critiques of theories of use under major evaluation theorists, Shadish, Cook, and Leviton (1991) repeatedly refer to short-term instrumental use and long-term enlightenment use. Although these are clear—and perhaps common—combinations of use within a results-based framework, the time dimension should be examined separately from nature of influence for maximum clarity.

A key point that is relevant to the conceptualization of the time dimension is whether use is seen as a point-in-time event or as a more open-ended process. Early definitions spoke of utilization as an event. For example, Alkin, Daillak, and White (1979) asked, "How do we know a utilization when we see one?" and "How do we define a utilization occurrence" (p. 226)? Their model of utilization culminated in "an instance of utilization" (p. 232). Leviton and Hughes (1981) used this same language, asking, "What is an instance of utilization?" (p. 533) frame one of four methodological issues in the study of utilization, unit of analysis. The language was shifting elsewhere from viewing utilization as a discrete instance to seeing it as an open-ended process. In changing terms from *utilization* to *use,* Weiss (1981) pointed to the need to move away from utilization as an event, which she illustrated by saying that utilizing evaluation was unlike utilizing a hammer. Cronbach (1982) viewed use as process, not as a point in time. He positioned evaluations as "part of the continuing accumulation of social knowledge" (p. 318). Fortunately, the delineation of periods within time does not presume use as an event, nor does it require resolution of the point-in-time versus process distinction. The time dimension directs attention to any influence that is visible in a given time period, whether it is an event occurring only within that period or a process that is flowing through it.[3]

Immediate Influence. Immediate influence refers to influence that occurs or is visible concurrent with the evaluation process. Immediate influence may occur during the process of anticipating, planning, and implementing evaluation. It includes early influences that plant the seeds of long-term effects or that may show cumulative impact over time as well as short-term effects that may not have long-term ramifications. Although it is the proponents of participatory, empowerment, and collaborative models who have, in their respective ways, brought this to our attention, immediate influence is not tied exclusively to these models. Witness, for example, the influence of accreditation on a program in preparation for and during the site visit process, preceding the delivery of judgment affirming or denying accreditation for that cycle. At first blush, immediate influence may be seen as exclusively process based; however, careful reflection on the variety of data that constitute results suggests that results-based use may also occur concurrent with the evaluation process. Evaluability assessment, for example, makes explicit the agenda of preparing systems for evaluation (Wholey, 1994). Adjustments made by a system in response to evaluability data during the assessment process represent immediate, intended, results-based influence.

Two clarifications are appropriate here. First, immediate influence is not necessarily fast paced. Because it is tied to the time frame of the evaluation, a slowly emerging evaluation effort that spans a period of months or even years could have a protracted period in which immediate influence could be examined. Second, the designation *immediate* does not speak to the duration of the influence. One could have an immediate influence that was short-lived or one that continued beyond the evaluation cycle and remained visible in subsequent time periods.

End-of-Cycle Influence. End-of-cycle influence highlights the influence surrounding the conclusion of a summative evaluation study or of a cycle in a more formative evaluation. It includes influence that emanates from both the products of the evaluation (for example, reports, summaries, and other documents) and the process of disseminating results. It also includes the process that brings closure to a particular evaluation cycle in the absence of a formal written report and in the context of more developmental use (Patton, 1994, 1997).[4] End-of-cycle influence parallels the notion of end-of-treatment effects in outcome evaluation, drawing attention to the conclusion of an evaluation study or of a given cycle in an ongoing evaluation effort. These cyclical demarcations may represent developmental phases of the evaluation itself or may result from program exigencies such as funding cycles. As Patton (1997) has noted, closure may or may not include an evaluation report, though markers for ending a cycle may admittedly be less clear in the absence of such a product.

Brett, Hill-Mead, and Wu (this volume) provide especially clear examples of cycles within a broader context of ongoing evaluation. Although examinations of results-based use traditionally focused on this time frame, process-based influence is worthy of note during this time frame as well. Process-based influence in this time period would include the effects of networking interactions surrounding an evaluation's closure, wrap-up, or winding down. Brett, Hill-Mead, and Wu describe an end-of-cycle influence that bridges process and results when they note that the structured, data-oriented reflection of the quarterly synthesis process taught staff how to mentor corps members in goal setting for the following year. An integrated theory of influence also opens the lens to attend to end-of-cycle unintended influences that may emanate from either process or results.

Long-Term Influence. Long-term influence captures effects that may not be felt for a period of time or that evolve over time into extended impact. The explicit inclusion of future use is helpful in reminding evaluators not to stop short in their examination of the influence of their work. Although influence during the process of evaluating and reporting results is important, the most powerful impact of the work may not yet have emerged or be visible in that time frame, lying instead in a future context. Preskill and Torres's treatment of use as transformative learning (this volume) emphasizes the importance of a long-term perspective, viewing such learning as a continual process of dialogue and reflection that occurs incrementally over time. The first step toward tracking and empirically studying future impact is the recognition of its conceptual relevance to an integrated theory of influence.

The importance of understanding long-term influence has been argued from theoretical, ethical, and pragmatic perspectives (Alkin, 1990; Shulha and Cousins, 1997). Though the significance of long-term influence is well recognized (Huberman and Cox, 1990; Patton; 1986; Weiss, 1980), Shulha and Cousins (1997) found it to be noteworthy in its absence from empirical studies of use. "While research studies have reported—usually through relatively immediate and retrospective methods—the instrumental, cognitive, affective, and political consequences of evaluation, they typically do not track these dimensions over the long term. As a result, they fail to produce a comprehensive picture of personal/professional change in participants and cultural change in organizations" (p. 204).

Long-term influence recognizes that influence may be visible well beyond the end of a particular evaluation cycle. It cues evaluators to watch for the emergence of impacts that are chronologically more distant from the evaluation as well as to track earlier impacts over time. Long-term influence may be delayed, long lasting, or both. In the case of delayed influence, for example, evaluation results from a consumer satisfaction study may initially lie unused due to the press of other program demands. However, when the self-study for the next accreditation cycle is initiated several years later, the self-study team correctly recognizes the relevance of the data already collected, and they incorporate these data in the self-study. In the case of long-lasting influence, results may exert ongoing influence that dates from the evaluation process itself. Focus group data may have first been used to provide immediate feedback to program providers, then incorporated into the annual report that accompanies the program's funding cycle. Accountability is maintained and future program funding is secured or perhaps expanded. In this example of results-based influence, the same data that are exerting long-term influence previously reaped immediate and end-of-cycle effects. In a combined model, some long-term influence continues from earlier time periods and some emerges for the first time. If, in the prior example, the focus group data were also used in community outreach efforts undertaken some time after the evaluation, this delayed influence would be added to the long-lasting influence previously described.

Summary. Attention to the timing of evaluation use is not new, though historically, discussions of time were often conflated with other dimensions rather than addressed explicitly. Early discussions of time focused on immediate use, with more recent attention underscoring the importance of long-term use. Similarly, early conceptualizations spoke of use as an event, whereas more recent discussions position use as a process. Dividing the time dimension into immediate, end-of-cycle, and long-term expands the common short-term versus long-term dichotomy and parallels conventional chronological description of program outcomes. The incremental nature of influence should not be obscured by the demarcation of three time periods, however. The intent is to cue consideration of a full range of influence across time rather than restricting reflection to a narrow band. Hence the time dimension helps one attend to both the pace of change and the chronological periods in which it is evidenced.

Utility of an Integrated Theory of Influence

This chapter has proposed an integrated theory of influence that conceptualizes evaluation influence in three dimensions—source, intention, and time. Source addresses results-based influence and process-based influence. Intention addresses unintended and intended influence. Time addresses influence that occurs during evaluation, at the end of evaluation, and in the future. These subcategories are not mutually exclusive. Together they portray influence as nonlinear and multifaceted, with broader roots than previously recognized.

An integrated theory of influence addresses fragmentation by creating a more expansive canvas against which to map influence. Interweaving disparate conversations of evaluation influence creates opportunities for valuable synergy of perspectives. Though it does not inherently eliminate the potential pitfalls of a factorial approach (Greene, 1988b), neither does it preclude a holistic approach to the study of influence. In fact, it demands a move away from a linear, simplistic representation of the relationship among evaluation, user, and affected person or system. The recognition that influence is multidirectional and interactive repositions the notion of "users" and "impactees." (See chapters by Rossman and Rallis and by Shulha for further discussion of repositioned evaluator and user roles.)

An integrated theory of influence contributes to the theory, practice, and study of evaluation in a number of ways. This closing section identifies nine potential applications of an integrated theory of influence.

Clarify debates on use. Through decades of explicit and implicit debates on use, evaluators representing different paradigms and application areas have frequently talked past one another, differences in terminology obscuring effective theory-building dialogue. Advancing the dialogue requires clarifying the assumptions that underlie the debates on use (Smith and Chircop, 1989). This theory of influence provides a framework for such clarification, one capacious enough to incorporate different evaluation paradigms and encourage the inspection of language and meaning.

Map influence surrounding a particular evaluation. For evaluation practitioners, the theory creates a framework to identify and map the types of influence that surround a particular evaluation. During evaluation planning and implementation, for example, evaluators can identify early effects that are associated with the process, whether or not they were intended. The case of City Year (Brett, Hill-Mead, and Wu, this volume) richly illustrates the varieties of evaluation influence on different systems levels across stages of program development.

Track evolving patterns of influence over time. This theory of influence cues evaluators to look beyond the end of a particular study and to examine evolving patterns of influence over time. One could track the long-term ramifications of an influence that had been observed in earlier time periods or could scan for evidence of late-emerging influence.

Sort out use and misuse. Whereas evaluation theory seeks to conceptualize use, meta-evaluation scrutinizes the appropriateness of use. The theory of influence proposed here supports meta-evaluation by laying a more comprehensive descriptive foundation. Discussions of misuse and misevaluation have been fraught with conceptual complexity and limited by a narrow image of use (see, for example, Alkin, 1990; Christie and Alkin, 1999). Little agreement has been reached on the relationship between use and misuse, and the parameters of misuse itself are often less than clear. Exploring source, intention, and time can expand conversations on misuse and illuminate beneficial and detrimental consequences of influence.

Improve validity of studies of influence. By integrating three dimensions of influence, this theory corrects the construct underrepresentation that weakened the validity of prior models of use. An integrated theory can improve empirical studies of utilization, such as those proposed by Conner (1998), by more fully specifying the dependent variable or by more clearly delimiting which dimensions of influence are to be addressed.

Facilitate meta-analysis of studies of influence. Historically, meta-analysis of empirical studies of use has been hampered by multiple definitions of the dependent variable (Conner, 1981; Cousins and Leithwood, 1986; Leviton and Hughes, 1981). Consideration of a more differentiated definition of influence may result in comparable studies for meta-analysis.

Track evolution of evaluation theory. The theory of influence provides a useful framework for more clearly understanding the evolution of a given theoretical approach. For example, Patton's utilization-focused evaluation has evolved from a singular focus on increasing the quality and quantity of results-based use to the recognition of process use in its own right (Patton, 1978, 1986, 1997, 1998). By examining the source, intention, and time frame of influence, one can more fully appreciate the evolutionary development of Patton's theory.

Compare evaluation theories. For evaluation theorists, this theory of influence promotes comparison among theories. Shadish, Cook, and Leviton (1991) have demonstrated the value of mapping and comparing evaluation theories. Their particular model addressed only results-based use, however. This integrated theory expands on their tradition by suggesting a more fully articulated examination of influence, permitting more fine-grained comparisons across theories. For example, evaluation as transformative learning (Preskill and Torres, this volume) could be compared with evaluation as sense making under emergent realist evaluation theory (Julnes and Mark, 1998) and with evaluation as critical inquiry (Rossman and Rallis, this volume), all of which involve influence via an iterative process of ongoing dialogue.

Support theory building. This theory of influence supports theory building and empirical study of utilization. It offers a framework for studying why evaluation may exert a particular influence under certain conditions, contributing to empirical tests of evaluation theory and furthering theory development. For example, this theory could be used to test Shulha's hypothesis (this volume) that evaluation and evaluation inquiry exhibit different patterns of influence or to extend the work of theorists such as Johnson (1998) to differentiate logic models underlying specific types of influence.

In closing, it is important to recognize how a more inclusive view of evaluation influence has positive implications for the evaluation profession as a whole (Shulha and Cousins, 1997). Although construct underrepresentation has been previously addressed as a validity issue, its pragmatic effect is that evaluation influence is underestimated. As construct underrepresentation is corrected, not only does validity improve, but also the full scope of evaluation influence becomes increasingly visible. For example, understanding long-term evaluation impact builds credibility for the profession and generates support for evaluation among service delivery professionals. This integrated theory of influence helps us recognize that evaluation practice has had a more pervasive impact than heretofore perceived.

Notes

1. The first two dimensions were addressed by Kirkhart (1995). The model presented here reflects a revision of that earlier work. This chapter is the product of many thoughtful conversations among the coauthors of this volume, energetic debates with early collaborators David M. Fetterman, Jean A. King, and William R. Shadish Jr., and continuing dialogue with Nick L. Smith.

2. Here the term *developmental* is used to acknowledge that these distinctions are not defined by the passage of time alone. They also stand in relation to the evaluation process, which itself moves through stages. For example, end-of-cycle influence is tied to the length of an evaluation cycle, not fixed at a certain number of weeks or months.

3. The logic here is analogous to that underlying interval recording procedures (Bloom, Fischer, and Orme, 1999). A time period is taken as the frame of reference, and any activity of interest—in this case, influence—that occurs during that interval is noted. When one shifts one's attention to a subsequent time period, evidence of influence would be noted again, even if it represented a continuation from the previous interval.

4. Although developmental use can occur within and across the time frames discussed in this chapter, Patton's (1997) example of developmental evaluation as reflective practice provides a clear instance of end-of-cycle influence. He describes a reflective cycle in which an issue is identified, a response is tried, the trial is observed, observations are reported and reflected on, patterns and themes are identified, action implications are determined, and the process is repeated. Note that this example includes data-based reflection, bridging process use and results-based use.

References

Alkin, M. C. *Debates on Evaluation.* Thousand Oaks, Calif.: Sage, 1990.

Alkin, M. C., Daillak, R., and White, P. *Using Evaluations: Does It Make a Difference?* Thousand Oaks, Calif.: Sage, 1979.

Anderson, C. D., Ciarlo, J. A., and Brodie, S. F. "Measuring Evaluation-Induced Change in Mental Health Programs." In J. A. Ciarlo (ed.), *Utilizing Evaluation: Concepts and Measurement Techniques.* Thousand Oaks, Calif.: Sage, 1981.

Anderson, S. B., and Ball, S. *The Profession and Practice of Program Evaluation.* San Francisco: Jossey-Bass, 1978.

Argyris, C., Putnam, R., and Smith, D. M. *Action Science.* San Francisco: Jossey-Bass, 1985.

Bloom, M., Fischer, J., and Orme, J. M. *Evaluating Practice: Guidelines for the Accountable Professional.* (3rd ed.) Needham Heights, Mass.: Allyn & Bacon, 1999.

Brisolara, S. "The History of Participatory Evaluation and Current Debates in the Field." In E. Whitmore (ed.), *Understanding and Practicing Participatory Evaluation.* New Directions for Evaluation, no. 80. San Francisco: Jossey-Bass, 1998.

Caro, F. G. "Leverage and Evaluation Effectiveness." *Evaluation and Program Planning,* 1980, *3*(2), 83–89.

Christie, C. A., and Alkin, M. C. "Further Reflections on Evaluation Misutilization." *Studies in Educational Evaluation,* 1999, *25,* 1–10.

Ciarlo, J. A. "Editor's Introduction." In J. A. Ciarlo (ed.), *Utilizing Evaluation: Concepts and Measurement Techniques.* Thousand Oaks, Calif.: Sage, 1981.

Conner, R. F. "Measuring Evaluation Utilization: A Critique of Different Techniques." In J. A. Ciarlo (ed.), *Utilizing Evaluation: Concepts and Measurement Techniques.* Thousand Oaks, Calif.: Sage, 1981.

Conner, R. F. "Toward a Social Ecological View of Evaluation Use." *American Journal of Evaluation,* 1998, *19*(2), 237–241.

Cousins, J. B., and Leithwood, K. A. "Current Empirical Research on Evaluation Utilization." *Review of Educational Research,* 1986, *56*(3), 331–364.

Cousins, J. B., and Whitmore, E. "Framing Participatory Evaluation." In E. Whitmore (ed.), *Understanding and Practicing Participatory Evaluation.* New Directions for Evaluation, no. 80. San Francisco: Jossey-Bass, 1998.

Cronbach, L. J. *Designing Evaluations of Educational and Social Programs.* San Francisco: Jossey-Bass, 1982.

Cronbach, L. J., and Associates. *Toward Reform of Program Evaluation: Aims, Methods, and Institutional Arrangements.* San Francisco: Jossey-Bass, 1980.

Fetterman, D. M. "Empowerment Evaluation." *Evaluation Practice,* 1994, *15*(1), 1–15.

Greene, J. C. "Communication of Results and Utilization in Participatory Program Evaluation." *Evaluation and Program Planning,* 1988a, *11*(4), 341–351.

Greene, J. C. "Stakeholder Participation and Utilization in Program Evaluation." *Evaluation Review,* 1988b, *12*(2), 91–116.

Henry, G. T., and Rog, D. J. "A Realist Theory and Analysis of Utilization." In G. T. Henry, G. Julnes, and M. M. Mark (eds.), *Realist Evaluation: An Emerging Theory in Support of Practice.* New Directions for Evaluation, no. 78. San Francisco: Jossey-Bass, 1998.

Hopson, R. K. "Editor's Notes." In R. K. Hopson (ed.), *How and Why Language Matters in Evaluation.* New Directions for Evaluation, no. 86. San Francisco: Jossey-Bass, 2000.

Huberman, M., and Cox, P. "Evaluation Utilization: Building Links Between Action and Reflection." *Studies in Educational Evaluation,* 1990, *16,* 157–179.

Johnson, R. B. "Toward a Theoretical Model of Evaluation Utilization." *Evaluation and Program Planning,* 1998, *21*(1), 93–110.

Julnes, G., and Mark, M. "Evaluation as Sensemaking: Knowledge Construction in a Realist World." In G. T. Henry, G. Julnes, and M. M. Mark (eds.), *Realist Evaluation: An Emerging Theory in Support of Practice.* New Directions for Evaluation, no. 78. San Francisco: Jossey-Bass, 1998.

Kirkhart, K. E. "Consequential Validity and an Integrated Theory of Use." Paper presented at Evaluation 1995, international evaluation conference cosponsored by the Canadian Evaluation Society and the American Evaluation Association, Vancouver, B.C., November 1995.

Kirkhart, K. E. " Multifaceted Dimensions of Use: Intended and Unintended Influences." Paper presented at the annual meeting of the American Evaluation Association, Orlando, Fla., Nov. 1999.

Knorr, K. D. "Policymakers' Use of Social Science Knowledge: Symbolic or Instrumental?" In C. H. Weiss (ed.), *Using Social Research in Public Policy Making*. Lexington, Mass.: Heath, 1977.

Leviton, L. C., and Hughes, E.F.X. "Research on the Utilization of Evaluations: A Review and Synthesis." *Evaluation Review*, 1981, 5(4), 525–548.

McClintock, C., and Colosi, L. A. "Evaluation of Welfare Reform: A Framework for Addressing the Urgent and the Important." *Evaluation Review*, 1998, 22(5), 668–694.

Messick, S. "Validity of Psychological Assessment: Validation of Inferences from Persons' Responses and Performance as Scientific Inquiry into Score Meaning." *American Psychologist*, 1995, 50(9), 741–749.

Mushkin, S. J. "Evaluations: Use with Caution." *Evaluation*, 1973, 1(2), 30–35.

Patton, M. Q. *Utilization-Focused Evaluation*. Thousand Oaks, Calif.: Sage, 1978.

Patton, M. Q. *Utilization-Focused Evaluation*. (2nd ed.) Thousand Oaks, Calif.: Sage, 1986.

Patton, M. Q. "Developmental Evaluation." *Evaluation Practice*, 1994, 15(3), 311–319.

Patton, M. Q. *Utilization-Focused Evaluation: The New Century Text*. (3rd ed.) Thousand Oaks, Calif.: Sage, 1997.

Patton, M. Q. "Discovering Process Use." *Evaluation*, 1998, 4(2), 225–233.

Patton, M. Q. "Overview: Language Matters." In R. K. Hopson (ed.), *How and Why Language Matters in Evaluation*. New Directions for Evaluation, no. 86. San Francisco: Jossey-Bass, 2000.

Preskill, H., and Caracelli, V. J. "Current and Developing Conceptions of Use: Evaluation Use Topical Interest Group Survey Results." *Evaluation Practice*, 1997, 18(3), 209–225.

Rein, M., and White, S. H. "Can Policy Research Help Policy?" *Public Interest*, 1975, 49, 119–136.

Rich, R. F. "Use of Social Science Information by Federal Bureaucrats: Knowledge for Action Versus Knowledge for Understanding." In C. H. Weiss (ed.), *Using Social Research in Public Policy Making*. Lexington, Mass.: Heath, 1977.

Rippey, R. M. (ed.). *Studies in Transactional Evaluation*. Berkeley, Calif.: McCutchan, 1973.

Rodman, H., and Kolodny, R. "Organizational Strains in the Researcher-Practitioner Relationship." In C. H. Weiss (ed.), *Evaluating Action Programs: Readings in Social Action and Education*. Needham Heights, Mass.: Allyn & Bacon, 1972.

Scriven, M. *Evaluation Thesaurus*. (4th ed.) Thousand Oaks, Calif.: Sage, 1991.

Shadish, W. R., Jr., Cook, T. D., and Leviton, L. C. *Foundations of Program Evaluation: Theories of Practice*. Thousand Oaks, Calif.: Sage, 1991.

Shulha, L. M., and Cousins, J. B. "Evaluation Use: Theory, Research, and Practice Since 1986." *Evaluation Practice*, 1997, 18(3), 195–208.

Smith, M. F. "Evaluation Utilization Revisited." In J. A. McLaughlin, L. J. Weber, R. W. Covert, and R. B. Ingle (eds.), *Evaluation Utilization*. New Directions for Program Evaluation, no. 39. San Francisco: Jossey-Bass, 1988.

Smith, N. L., and Chircop, S. "The Weiss-Patton Debate: Illumination of the Fundamental Concerns." *Evaluation Practice*, 1989, 10(1), 5–13.

Suchman, E. A. *Evaluative Research: Principles and Practice in Public Service and Social Action Programs*. New York: Russell Sage Foundation, 1967.

Tornatzky, L. G. "The Triple-Threat Evaluator." *Evaluation and Program Planning*, 1979, 2(2), 111–115.

Weiss, C. H. "Knowledge Creep and Decision Accretion." *Knowledge: Creation, Utilization, Diffusion*, 1980, 1(3), 381–404.

Weiss, C. H. "Measuring the Use of Evaluation." In J. A. Ciarlo (ed.), *Utilizing Evaluation: Concepts and Measurement Techniques*. Thousand Oaks, Calif.: Sage, 1981.

Weiss, C. H., and Bucuvalas, M. J. "Truth Tests and Utility Tests: Decision-Makers' Frames of Reference for Social Science Research." *American Sociological Review*, 1980, 45, 302–313.

Whitmore, E. "Evaluation and Empowerment: It's the Process That Counts." *Empowerment and Family Support Networking Bulletin* (Cornell University Empowerment Project), 1991, 2(2), 1–7.

Wholey, J. S. "Assessing the Feasibility and Likely Usefulness of Evaluation." In J. S. Wholey, H. P. Hatry, and K. E. Newcomer (eds.), *Handbook of Practical Program Evaluation*. San Francisco: Jossey-Bass, 1994.

KAREN E. KIRKHART is professor of social work at Syracuse University. Her interests include evaluation and social justice and the validity of evaluation in multicultural contexts.

2

Evaluation's role in facilitating transformative learning in organizations is the focus of this chapter. The theories underlying constructivist and transformative learning, as well as specific evaluator roles and practices to support it, are described.

The Learning Dimension
of Evaluation Use

Hallie Preskill, Rosalie T. Torres

We are encouraged by many of the arguments made by authors in this volume about the need for not only an integrated theory of evaluation use but also a reconceptualization of what use means in organizations, communities, and society. We agree with Kirkhart (Chapter One) that a theory of use is long overdue and that traditional perspectives of use do not account for the more transformative goals of several contemporary evaluation approaches.

Our evaluation ideas embrace these transformative goals. Specifically, we are interested in the use of evaluation to facilitate learning—especially *transformative learning* in organizational contexts. In reference to Kirkhart's three-dimensional framework of evaluation influence, our construal of influence is anchored in *intentional uses of the evaluation process over time,* but in application it may also include unintentional uses of the evaluation findings. Our focus is on the learning that occurs through the evaluative process—learning about job processes, the diverse perspectives of different coworkers, organizational culture, personal understanding, and the like. This focus includes learning at the individual, team, and organization levels. We argue that such learning can be advanced through an evaluative process that is collaborative, dialogic, and action oriented.

We first briefly review the history of evaluation use and then discuss the increasing need for organizations to focus on *constructivist* and transformative learning. As we consider the meaning and value of constructivist and transformative learning theories, we relate how a collaborative and dialogic evaluation approach helps operationalize these theories. The second half of this chapter focuses on the role of evaluators and specific evaluation practices that promote transformative learning in organizations.

NEW DIRECTIONS FOR EVALUATION, no. 88, Winter 2000   © Jossey-Bass

Evaluation Use

Evaluation use has been of interest to evaluators and funders of evaluation work since the beginnings of the evaluation profession. For over three decades, the guiding assumption has been that evaluations are conducted to provide information for use in decision making. Prompted by U.S. congressional members' criticism in the late 1960s that evaluation results were not being used, evaluation researchers fervently sought to better understand the full range of evaluation use, including instances of use that were not immediately discernible. As a result, three categories of use were identified—instrumental, conceptual, and symbolic (or political or persuasive) (Leviton and Hughes, 1981). In the 1970s and 1980s, a great deal of research was conducted to try to identify the factors related to increased levels of use (see Alkin, Daillak, and White, 1979; Cousins and Leithwood, 1986; Patton, 1986). Most, if not all, of these studies, however, focused on the use of evaluation *findings* or as Kirkhart (Chapter One) labels them, results-based uses.

In the last several years, there has been growing interest in expanding the notion of evaluation use beyond the intended use of findings. Several evaluators have written about the importance and value of involving various stakeholders in the evaluation process and have discussed the benefits of such participation (Cousins and Earl, 1992, 1995; Fetterman, 1994; Greene, 1988; Patton, 1994; Preskill, 1994; Torres and Preskill, 1999a). In 1997, Patton labeled the learning that occurs from such participation *process use,* which he defines as "individual changes in thinking and behavior, and program or organizational changes in procedures and culture, that occur among those involved in evaluation as a result of the learning that occurs during the evaluation process. Evidence of process use is represented by the following kind of statement after an evaluation: 'The impact on our program came not just from the findings but from going through the thinking process that the evaluation required'" (p. 90).

Others have described this kind of use as a form of individual, team, and organizational learning (Cousins and Earl, 1992; Jenlink, 1994; Owen and Lambert, 1995; Preskill, 1994; Preskill and Torres, 1999a; Torres, Preskill, and Piontek, 1996). These authors suggest that when individuals participate in an evaluation process that is collaborative and guided by dialogue and reflection, learning occurs not only at the individual level but also at the team and organization levels.

The literature on evaluation use shows that the concept has evolved considerably over the last several years to its current focus on learning that arises from participating in evaluation activities (see Preskill and Caracelli, 1997). As Shulha and Cousins (1997) conclude in their review of evaluation use since 1986, "We underscore that many of the authors cited . . . are committed to models of joint participation in making meaning, opportunities for invested authority, and the potential for long term, productive learning partnerships. While the specific skill set required to move into this realm is vast and complex, the learning—often acquired 'on the fly'—for both evaluators and program practitioners/users has considerable allure" (p. 205). This expanded view positions evaluation as a mechanism for facilitating learning in organizations. In the following section, we discuss the increasing need for organizations to focus on learning.

Learning in Organizations

"When people are learning, whether it's personally or professionally, they are growing. This growth equates to workers' job advancement, satisfaction, and self-esteem. Companies that invest in continuous learning by their employees are positioning themselves for success in the future" (Herman and Gioia, 1998, p. 12). Increasingly, organizations are recognizing that employee learning is essential to their success. As organizations strive to remain viable in today's volatile marketplace, they continue to search for ways to improve the delivery and management of employee learning.

Workplace learning has traditionally been undertaken to support the accomplishment of *tasks*, requiring employees to work independently, make logic-based decisions, act quickly, focus on details, keep things moving, control outside influences, and tell other people what and how to do their work. But today's knowledge-based work environment emphasizes *processes*, requiring employees to focus on thinking; work in teams; use creativity and innovation; talk, explore ideas; think holistically; facilitate; empower others; ask questions; focus on people, values, and vision; and be more open to change (Bendaly, 1999). These kinds of processes are the mainstay of transformative learning. They include employee participation in "task forces, problem-solving teams or quality circles; job rotation or cross training; and employee access to key business information" to accomplish their work (McMurrer, Van Buren, and Woodwell, 2000, p. 21).

The challenge for organizations is to figure out how to embrace this kind of change in a way that allows them to move forward without abandoning what has worked in the past. As organizations seek ways to enhance employee learning, they are looking beyond the formal classroom and more toward the informal learning mechanisms that bring employees together (Watkins and Marsick, 1992). We believe that this situation offers evaluation a unique opportunity—a means for helping individuals, teams, and organizations learn from their past and current practices. Such learning will most likely occur when organization members engage in collaborative, dialogic, and reflective forms of evaluation practice (Preskill and Torres, 1999a). Before we discuss the specific evaluator roles and practices that promote constructivist and transformative learning, it is important to clearly understand what we mean by this type of learning and the evaluation approach it requires.

Constructivist and Transformative Learning

Although the task-focused perspective of workplace learning may be adequate for some employee skills training, a growing number of adult-learning theorists argue that this view contributes little to understanding the learning needs of employees whose jobs are constantly changing (Marsick and Volpe, 1999). An increasingly preferred perspective is constructivist learning theory, which views learning as a process of meaning making (Brookfield, 1991; Brooks and Brooks, 1993; Cranton, 1994; Dirkx, 1998; Jackson and MacIssac, 1994; Jarvis, 1992; Mezirow, 1991). Constructivist learning theory suggests that individuals and groups learn by interpreting, understanding, and making sense of their experiences, often within a social context. Learners are not passive (as implied in behaviorism models of learning) but rather active participants in the construction of their own knowledge and the use of that knowledge in their work.

When organization members are provided with opportunities for constructivist learning, they are often transformed by their experiences. The transformation represents "a break with existing routines and a shift to new competencies that challenge previous knowledge and beliefs" (Aldrich, 1999, p. 165). In the work context, transformational learning theory focuses on the transactional relationship between the work and the self (Dirkx, 1998). Such learning involves identifying, acquiring, examining, questioning, validating, and revising information in order that individuals in an organization meet their goals (Cranton, 1994; Tobin, 1996). Creating opportunities for transformative learning in the workplace, and especially from evaluation, requires that employees work through differing perceptions, beliefs, and attitudes instead of assuming that they do not exist or intentionally ignoring them (Hobson and Welbourne, 1998). The most significant transformative learning occurs when the purpose is to understand what others mean and to make ourselves understood. This most often "arises spontaneously within the context of real work" (Marsick and Volpe, 1999, p. 4).

The notion of developing *communities of practice* has recently been described as a method for bringing people together to facilitate the work and learning of employees (Brown and Duguid, 1991; Lave and Wenger, 1991; Wenger, 1998). Communities of practice are places where organization members participate in common practices, depend on one another, make decisions together, identify themselves as part of something larger than the sum of their individual relationships, and commit themselves to their own and the group's well-being. Such communities are made up of individuals who typically come together voluntarily, drawn by a common social and professional force (Tetenbaum and Tetenbaum, 2000; Wenger, 1998). Even though these communities are often assembled to address some issue, the effect is that "problem-solving becomes more of a social activity than an analytically detached process" (Raelin, 2000, p. 75). Specifically, communities of practice are most effective when they

- Have the time and space for learning
- Pay attention to goals and significant organizational events
- Have accurate and complete information
- Are able to weigh evidence and assess arguments
- Are open to alternative perspectives
- Reflect critically on presuppositions and their consequences
- Trust the process of working with others
- Are able to accept an informed, objective, and rational consensus as a legitimate test of validity
- Take action on organizational issues (Marsick and Volpe, 1999; Mezirow, 1991; Watkins and Marsick, 1992)

Though the authors who have written about constructivist, transformative, and informal learning and communities of practice do not use the term *evaluation* to describe the role of information gathering and problem solving in organizations, we believe that the implications for evaluation are clear. Learning from evaluation and from organization members' subsequent use of what they learn will most likely occur when evaluation is collaborative, is grounded in constructivist and transformational learning theories, and builds communities of evaluation practice. A constructivist and transformational perspective on workplace learning—much like collaborative, participatory, and empowerment approaches to evaluation—is based on the belief that learning is "inherently communal, dialogical and cooperative" (Leitch, Harrison, and Burgoyne, 1996, p. 3).

Evaluation Roles and Practices for Transformative Learning

Transformative learning can be facilitated when employees seek to understand something, address critical organizational issues, and improve their work through a participatory, dialogic, reflective, and inquiry-oriented approach to evaluation and the use of findings. Our view of this kind of evaluation approach features three interrelated aspects of an evaluator's role and practice—using a clinical approach, spanning traditional program and evaluation boundaries, and helping diagnose an organization's capacity for learning. This section discusses these roles and practices and concludes with implications for internal and external evaluator roles.

Using a Clinical Approach. The capacity of the evaluator to provide technical assistance in design, methods, and data analysis is a necessary but insufficient condition for success in facilitating transformative learning. Collaborative, dialogic, and reflective forms of evaluation practice are best supported through a clinical approach practiced by evaluators who understand how transformative learning occurs in organizations and where it can be developed. A clinical approach to evaluation is both highly customized and evolutionary, taking shape over time. In particular, it focuses on the current needs, context and history, and changing circumstances of a program or organization. The following discussion describes three aspects of a clinical approach to evaluation practice that supports transformative learning.

Viewing Learning as Incremental and Iterative. First and foremost is the recognition that the processes that lead to transformative learning are both incremental and iterative—that is, learning at the individual and group levels builds on past learning and experiences over time. This point is particularly important because use needs to be considered along a continuum of time—from the beginning of an evaluation's design to several months or even years after it has been completed (see Kirkhart, Chapter One, for a more detailed discussion of evaluation use and the time dimension).

Internal evaluators with more continual access to organization members and external evaluators who are engaged in multiyear work with clients likely have the greatest opportunities to facilitate transformative learning. Abiding contact with evaluation audiences means that evaluators can continually scan for *teachable moments* as well as actively plan for specific opportunities to facilitate learning. An example of the latter occurs when, at the outset of any new evaluation effort, program staff review what is known about the evaluand from previous inquiries and then connect what is already known to new information being sought. This is a particularly useful dialogue because the *results* of earlier evaluation studies are often forgotten with the passage of time, especially when competing priorities for individuals' time have precluded extensive discussion and consideration of available findings. When organization members fail to review previous findings, they may start anew asking questions that have already been addressed. In contrast, new evaluations that build on previous inquiries can result in deeper and stronger understandings of complex phenomena. Such successive iterations over time produce results that more and more closely approximate the desired result—transformative learning.

Another way to capitalize on the iterative nature of transformative learning is to begin any new inquiries by examining the evaluation *processes* of previous studies. Thus organization members can pay particular attention to what either facilitated or inhibited the success of the evaluation. The following questions may help individuals reflect on what they have learned from previous evaluation studies:

- What kinds of data does the organization typically respond to? What does it ignore?
- To what extent was the type of data from previous studies considered credible by the organization?

- What political issues related to the use of different data collection methods have surfaced in the past?
- How might the answers to any of these questions influence decision making about the present inquiry (Preskill and Torres, 1999a)?

Although internal evaluators would most readily have access to this information, external evaluators can also pursue these questions at the outset of their work with organizations.

Using Responsive Methods. Clinical approaches are inherently responsive to the needs of the organization and its members. And indeed it is any evaluator's primary job to help clients select and use evaluation methods that will generate the most valid and reliable data given existing logistical, resource, and even political constraints (Torres, 1991). Being highly responsive also means that an evaluator can help identify those instances when compromising on methodological rigor may be worth considering, such as those times when doing so will yield information that is not otherwise available and that can be used as a basis for dialogue, reflection, and learning.

Under some circumstances, having some data to inform an issue or concern may well be better than having none. An example of such a circumstance is when the stakes surrounding an evaluation effort are not high and the liabilities of a less-than-ideal methodology can be managed. A clinical approach that uses responsive methods allows for more flexibility in such situations. In these cases, dialogue and reflection among evaluation users must allow for full consideration of the methodological limitations, interpretations should be mediated accordingly, and the risk of misinterpretation by outside audiences must be minimal to nonexistent. When using limited data, dialogue, reflection, and sense making can support transformational learning, even if it is primarily about understanding and prioritizing the resources necessary to conduct more thorough evaluations.

Another way of using a responsive methodology comes in exercising judgment about the level of analysis and presentation of data that will be maximally useful to (that is, easily assimilated by) organization members. Communicating and reporting formats that are designed for use in working sessions where findings are presented and then discussed can result in greater learning than written reports and one-way verbal presentations. A typical challenge for successful working sessions is to present a substantial amount of complex data in a short period of time—such that organization members can grasp and use it in subsequent dialogue, reflection, and action planning. Social constructivist learning often happens when individuals are reviewing information together. Substantial use of graphics, posters, and other means of visual display that can be viewed by a group are useful for having those present "process" the data together rather than individually. Individuals are able to share their reactions, questions, and possibly their underlying values and assumptions as they collectively interpret the findings. As a result, transformative learning can occur for individuals and groups.

Articulating, Formalizing, and Making Time for Learning Processes. To wax eloquent about the processes of transformative learning as though they are rarefied and infrequent would be misleading. It is likely that transformative learning is occurring more often than we realize, particularly in group settings. For example, working sessions of several hours, or even the course of a day, in which a group has the opportunity to hear about evaluation findings, interpret them, construct meaning, and plan next steps provide opportunities for learning. However, finding the time to engage in such learning processes on a regular basis may not be easy for today's busy and overcommitted employees. Naming these processes and constructing conceptual frameworks to guide organization members in the use of evaluation findings and the processes of learning helps legitimize these activities and encourages busy people to give priority to the time that organizational learning requires. By continually revisiting where the group is in the learning process relative to the program or project being evaluated, the perception of having to make time for learning disappears because it becomes integrated with how work routinely gets done.

Spanning Traditional Boundaries. The role we are describing requires evaluators to be more regularly and intimately involved in the work of an organization, and in such a way that pushes up against the boundaries traditionally maintained between evaluation and program staff. In particular, these boundaries may become blurred as evaluators guide program staff in dialogue and reflection processes that initially focus on evaluation findings but then move into dialogues about the specifics of action planning. At its best, such work can be described as a "seamless blend of program work, research and evaluation, and organizational development" (Eric Schaps, personal communication, December 3, 1998). Acting in a facilitator role for this kind of dialogue may be new for some evaluators who have previously independently developed conclusions and recommendations and then delivered them to the evaluation client.

Spanning the evaluation-program boundary can be tricky. As evaluators work as facilitators of transformative learning, they become more knowledgeable about the work of the program or organization and may have more to offer in the way of ideas and observations about what findings mean and what specific steps can or should be taken to make program improvements. Yet if program staff perceive the evaluator as having an agenda with respect to the program's content or direction, or the outcomes of the evaluation, the evaluation process may become politicized and its credibility jeopardized. It is essential that program staff clearly understand the evaluator's role in this capacity and are comfortable with it. Typically, this credibility and comfort arises from evaluators' exercising sound professional judgment and building solid and thoughtful relationships with program staff.

As a second example, some evaluators are spanning program and evaluation boundaries when they work with program staff to develop programmatic theories of action. The program's theory of action is often depicted as a logic model that delineates the relationships between and among program resources and program activities, intermediate states or outcomes, and the ultimate intended outcomes of the program (see Chen, 1990; Sidani and Sechrest, 1999; Trochim, 1989; Weiss, 1997). Indeed Weiss (1997) points out that when an evaluator adopts a theory-based approach, it is often because the evaluator is also the program developer and is working to develop, test, and modify the intervention. However, when the evaluators and the program developers and the staff are not the same, articulation of the program's theory of action can require substantial collaboration among the individuals or groups. This work, at least initially, focuses on the details and intended effects of program activities (and not on the means of evaluating them). Thereafter the theory of action can serve as a framework for continued evaluation of and dialogue about the program. It can help create a single shared, but evolving, understanding about what the program is, what the necessary conditions for its implementation are, and which part of it is being addressed by any given evaluation effort. Thus over time the development of the program's theory of action is informed by the program's underlying theory and rationale, as well as by evaluation findings. This process results in learning about the program's espoused theory compared with its theory in use (Argyris, 1992) and can provide detailed information about aligning the two.

Diagnosing Organizational Capacity for Learning from Evaluative Inquiry. Any truly successful clinical approach takes into account the context in which the evaluative inquiry is occurring, that is, the host organization's infrastructure—its culture, leadership, forms of communication, and systems and structures. Most evaluators attend to these infrastructure elements, at least informally, as they design and carry out their work. More formal assessment of the infrastructure, including assessing the extent to which organization members work in teams and the extent to which evaluation is already taking place, can inform both the organization and the evaluator about how readily evaluative inquiry efforts are likely to lead to transformative learning (Preskill and Torres, 1999b). Diagnosing which aspects of the organization's culture, leadership, forms of communication, and systems and structures are present to support evaluative inquiry and learning, and which are not, can help evaluators set realistic expectations for learning and refine and adapt their approach so as to maximize the likelihood of transformative learning.

For instance, through the use of a diagnostic instrument completed by all organization members, it might be determined that an organization's leadership and overall culture are only moderately supportive of organizational learning. In this case, debriefing these results with the organization would serve several purposes. First, it could make clear how undertaking evaluative inquiry to support workplace learning would most likely run counter to certain organizational norms and practices. Second, it could help both the evaluator and the organization see what efforts might be necessary to help ensure success—for example, scheduling time and creating an atmosphere in which values and assumptions about evaluation methods and findings can be examined freely. Third, it could help organization leaders understand how their practices and signals can promote the risk taking and self-examination that leads to individual, team, and organizational learning. Finally, this diagnosis can guide the evaluator in choosing the particular strategies, methods of communication, and stage setting that will be necessary to help ensure success.

Internal and External Evaluator Roles. Ultimately, evaluators have opportunities for a variety of roles as they work with programs, projects, and organizations. For internal evaluators, transformative learning through evaluation use may occur through long-term sustained interaction with organization members. The internal evaluator may be in an advantageous position to link specific program or departmental issues with larger organizational issues. And the longer any evaluator maintains a relationship with potential users, the greater the likelihood that long-term use may be observed (see Kirkhart, Chapter One). The key, however, is not so much whether an evaluator is internal or external but rather how the evaluator sees his or her role. Evaluators who view their role as facilitating transformative learning will operate as much as educators, consultants, interpreters, mediators, or even emancipators (see Torres, Preskill, and Piontek, 1996) as they do technical, expert-scientist researchers. Both internal and external evaluators need to assume an educative role in helping clients understand and appreciate the benefits of transformative learning and how evaluation can support it.

Conclusion

Interest in more collaborative and dialogic approaches to evaluation has already begun to influence both research and practice (see, for example, Minnet, 1999; Ryan and DeStefano, 2000; Wilkerson, 1999). As we begin to inquire more deeply into the various forms of evaluation practice that facilitate transformative learning, we are learning not only how evaluation findings are used but also how engaging in the evaluation process affects individuals and teams, as well as how evaluator roles are changing (see Torres and others, 2000).

Using evaluation as a catalyst for transformative learning invites us to view fewer and fewer influences of the evaluation as unintended (see Kirkhart, Chapter One). What is intended is learning—wherever that leads the organization and its constituents. It is not sufficient for organizations to merely conduct evaluation as an information-gathering activity. As Bendaly (1999) notes, "Knowing how to use [information] effectively is just as important. Organizations that . . . have and use the information that they need . . . know what information is required . . . will have made information scanning part of the job . . . know how to integrate information into organizational responses . . . and share information—including strategic information—and good and bad news quickly and openly" (p. 50).

Hobson and Welbourne (1998) suggest, "The route to transformation lies in acknowledging contradictions and differences and working through them, as opposed to ignoring or circumventing them" (p. 84). Evaluation that is collaborative, reflective, and dialogic is a mechanism for creating communities of evaluation practice that can take organization members down this path of learning, which is both intentional and transformative.

References

Aldrich, H. *Organizations Evolving.* Thousand Oaks, Calif.: Sage, 1999.

Alkin, M. C., Daillak, R., and White, P. *Using Evaluations: Does It Make a Difference?* Thousand Oaks, Calif.: Sage, 1979.

Argyris, C. *On Organizational Learning.* Cambridge, Mass.: Blackwell, 1992.

Bendaly, L. *Organization 2005.* Indianapolis, Ind.: Park Avenue Productions, 1999.

Brookfield, S. "The Development of Critical Reflection in Adulthood." *New Education,* 1991, *13*(1), 39–48.

Brooks, J. G., and Brooks, M. G. *In Search of Understanding: The Case of the Constructivist Classroom.* Alexandria, Va.: Association for Supervision and Curriculum Development, 1993.

Brown, J. S., and Duguid, P. "Organizational Learning and Communities-of-Practice." *Organization Science,* 1991, *2*(1).

Chen, H. T. *Theory-Driven Evaluations.* Thousand Oaks, Calif.: Sage, 1990.

Cousins, J. B., and Earl, L. M. "The Case for Participatory Evaluation." *Educational Evaluation and Policy Analysis,* 1992, *14*(4), 397–418.

Cousins, J. B., and Earl, L. M. "The Case for Participatory Evaluation: Theory, Research, Practice." In J. B. Cousins and L. M. Earl (eds.), *Participatory Evaluation in Education.* Bristol, Pa.: Falmer Press, 1995.

Cousins, J. B., and Leithwood, K. A. "Current Empirical Research on Evaluation Utilization." *Review of Educational Research,* 1986, *56*(3), 331–364.

Cranton, P. *Understanding and Promoting Transformative Learning.* San Francisco: Jossey-Bass, 1994.

Dirkx, J. M. "Knowing the Self Through Fantasy and Imagination: Implications for Adult Learning in the Context of Work." Paper presented at the Academy of Human Resource Development conference, Chicago, Mar. 1998.

Fetterman, D. M. "Empowerment Evaluation." *Evaluation Practice,* 1994, *15*(1), 1–15.

Greene, J. C. "Stakeholder Participation and Utilization in Program Evaluation." *Evaluation Review,* 1988, *12*(2), 91–116.

Herman, R. E., and Gioia, J. L. *Lean and Meaningful.* Winchester, Va.: Oakhill Press, 1998.

Hobson, P., and Welbourne, L. "Adult Development and Transformative Learning." *International Journal of Lifelong Education,* 1998, *17*(2), 72–86.

Jackson, L., and MacIssac, D. "Introducing a New Approach to Experiential Learning." In L. Jackson and R. S. Caffarella (eds.), *New Directions for Adult and Continuing Education,* 1994, *55*, 17–27.

Jarvis, P. *Paradoxes of Learning.* San Francisco: Jossey-Bass, 1992.

Jenlink, P. M. "Using Evaluation to Understand the Learning Architecture of an Organization." *Evaluation and Program Planning,* 1994, *17*, 3, pp. 315–325.

Lave, J., and Wenger, E. *Situated Learning: Legitimate Peripheral Participation.* Cambridge, England: Cambridge University Press, 1991.

Leitch, C., Harrison, R., and Burgoyne, J. "Understanding the Learning Company: A Constructivist Approach." Paper presented at the Organizational Learning Symposium, University of Lancaster, England, Sept. 1996.

Leviton, L. C., and Hughes, E.F.X. "Research on the Utilization of Evaluations: A Review and Synthesis." *Evaluation Review,* 1981, *5*(4), 525–548.

Marsick, V. J., and Volpe, M. "The Nature and Need for Informal Learning." In V. J. Marsick and M. Volpe (eds.), *Informal Learning on the Job.* San Francisco: Berrett- Koehler, 1999.

McMurrer, D. P., Van Buren, M. E., and Woodwell, W. H. Jr. *The 2000 American Society for Training and Development State of the Industry Report.* Alexandria, Va.: American Society for Training & Development, 2000.

Mezirow, J. *Transformative Dimensions of Adult Learning.* San Francisco: Jossey-Bass, 1991.

Minnet, A. M. "Internal Evaluation in a Self-Reflective Organization: One Nonprofit Agency's Model." *Evaluation and Program Planning,* 1999, *22*(3), 353–362.

Owen, J. M., and Lambert, F. C. "Roles for Evaluation in Learning Organisations." *Evaluation,* 1995, *1*(2), 259–273.

Patton, M. Q. *Utilization-Focused Evaluation.* (2nd ed.) Thousand Oaks, Calif.: Sage, 1986.

Patton, M. Q. "Developmental Evaluation." *Evaluation Practice,* 1994, *15*(3), 311–319.

Patton, M. Q. *Utilization-Focused Evaluation: The New Century Text.* (3rd ed.) Thousand Oaks, Calif.: Sage, 1997.

Preskill, H. "Evaluation's Role in Facilitating Organizational Learning: A Model for Practice." *Evaluation and Program Planning,* 1994, *17*(3), 291–298.

Preskill, H., and Caracelli, V. J. "Current and Developing Conceptions of Use: Evaluation Use Topical Interest Group Survey Results." *Evaluation Practice,* 1997, *18*(3), 209–225.

Preskill, H., and Torres, R. T. *Evaluative Inquiry for Learning in Organizations.* Thousand Oaks, Calif.: Sage, 1999a.

Preskill, H., and Torres, R. T. "Assessing an Organization's Readiness for Learning from Evaluative Inquiry." Paper presented at the annual meeting of the American Evaluation Association, Orlando, Nov. 1999b.

Raelin, J. A. *Work-Based Learning.* Englewood Cliffs, N.J.: Prentice Hall, 2000.

Ryan, K. E., and DeStefano, L. (eds.). *Evaluation as a Democratic Process: Promoting Inclusion, Dialogue, and Deliberation.* New Directions for Evaluation, no. 85. San Francisco: Jossey-Bass, 2000.

Shulha, L. M., and Cousins, J. B. "Evaluation Use: Theory, Research, and Practice Since 1986." *Evaluation Practice,* 1997, *18*(3), 195–208.

Sidani, S., and Sechrest, L. "Putting Program Theory into Operation." *American Journal of Evaluation,* 1999, *20*(2), 227–238.

Tetenbaum, T., and Tetenbaum, H. "Office 2000: Tear Down the Walls." *Training,* 2000, *37*(2), 58–64.

Tobin, D. R. *Transformational Learning.* New York: Wiley, 1996.

Torres, R. T. "Improving the Quality of Internal Evaluation: The Evaluator as Consultant-Mediator." *Evaluation and Program Planning,* 1991, *14*(3), 189–198.

Torres, R. T., and Preskill, H. "Ethical Dimensions of Stakeholder Participation and Evaluation Use." In J. L. Fitzpatrick and M. Morris (eds.), *Current and Emerging Ethical Challenges in Evaluation.* New Directions for Evaluation, no. 82. San Francisco: Jossey-Bass, 1999.

Torres, R. T., Preskill, H., and Piontek, M. *Evaluation Strategies for Communication and Reporting.* Thousand Oaks, Calif.: Sage, 1996.

Torres, R. T., and others. "Dialogue and Reflection in a Collaborative Evaluation: Stakeholder and Evaluator Voices." In K. E. Ryan and L. DeStefano (eds.), *Evaluation as a Democratic Process: Promoting Inclusion, Dialogue, and Deliberation.* New Directions for Evaluation, no. 85. San Francisco: Jossey-Bass, 2000.

Trochim, W. "An Introduction to Concept Mapping for Planning and Evaluation." *Evaluation and Program Planning,* 1989, *12,* 1–6.

Watkins, K. A., and Marsick, V. J. "Towards a Theory of Informal and Incidental Learning in Organizations." *International Journal of Lifelong Education,* 1992, *11,* 287–300.

Weiss, C. H. "Theory-Based Evaluation: Past, Present, and Future." In D. J. Rog and D. Fournier (eds.), *Progress and Future Directions in Evaluation: Perspectives on Theory, Practice, and Methods.* New Directions for Evaluation, no. 76. San Francisco: Jossey-Bass, 1997.

Wenger, E. *Communities of Practice: Learning, Meaning, and Identity.* Cambridge, England: Cambridge University Press, 1998.

Wilkerson, S. B. "Evaluation in a Learning Organization: Mid-Continent Research for Education and Learning (McREL) as a Case Study." Paper presented at the annual meeting of the American Evaluation Association, Orlando, Fla., Nov. 1999.

HALLIE PRESKILL is professor of organizational learning and instructional technologies in the College of Education at the University of New Mexico, Albuquerque. Her research and consulting work focus on developing evaluation learning communities.

ROSALIE T. TORRES is director of research and evaluation at the Developmental Studies Center in Oakland, California.

3

School-university partnerships with professional learning agendas provide appealing contexts for the introduction and application of systematic evaluative inquiry. The challenges faced by evaluators in moving from results-focused evaluation to learning-oriented evaluative inquiry are discussed, as are the influences of this transition on individual practitioners and their organizations.

Evaluative Inquiry in University-School Professional Learning Partnerships

Lyn M. Shulha

With the arrival of the information age, the viability of associations, institutions, and businesses has become increasingly dependent on their capacity to access reliable and valid data and then to understand, evaluate, and communicate the data's import. This subset of skills allows organizations to flourish in conditions that are dynamic, ambiguous, and loosely coupled. In contexts in which individuals and work groups are interdependent, members need to be confident that problem solving and decision making at all levels of the organization are being done skillfully and with due regard for both individual perspectives and organizational goals. There is evidence that when these skills are developed while responding to real workplace dilemmas, members are more likely to see their learning as natural personal and professional development. Preskill and Torres (this volume) describe this phenomenon as *workplace learning,* learning that is sometimes transformative in nature.

In schools, the capacity to work interdependently, reliably, and creatively with information is especially vital. The activities of curriculum design, instruction, student assessment, program planning, and policy development depend on it. At stake is no less than the effectiveness of schooling and the quality of learning experienced by students. In schools, however, it is rare to find the structures and resources necessary to support teachers and administrators in intentional and continual inquiry into programs and practices. Even when on-site professional learning agendas that use evaluation frameworks are attempted, they can be easily derailed by external political agendas, administrative agendas, and the normal business of schooling (King, 1995; Shulha and Wilson, 1995).

Professional development days and summer courses continue to be popular, informative and even inspirational for many educators. Yet, linkages between the knowledge and skills acquired in these ways and the experiences of teaching and learning in schools remains tenuous (Squire, 2000). Most problems in teaching and schooling present themselves not as well-formed independent structures but as messy and indeterminate situations shaped by the organization's policies, structures, culture, personnel, and clientele (Schön, 1987). Traditional professional development focuses on the delivery of common sets of learnings. Traditional assessment measures the degree to which these foundational ideas have been absorbed. It should not be surprising, therefore, when even the most successful participants in these types of professional development programs struggle with the task of transforming generalized learnings into usable working knowledge. This step requires educators to process their learning against the full array of contextual variables unique to the school. Professional learning that counts must enable educators to become adept at the information-use skills and dispositions that make it possible for new learnings to inform future individual and organizational practices.

This chapter proposes that when evaluative inquiry is established as the foundation for a school-university learning partnership, the result is a potent alternative to classical forms of professional development. A brief examination of more traditional school-university partnerships and the roles that evaluation has typically played in these partnerships will lead to the argument that a useful distinction can be made between evaluation and evaluative inquiry. A description of a needs assessment conducted by two evaluators and a work group of eighteen teachers from a potential partner school demonstrates some of the practical challenges of rooting a university-school learning partnership in evaluative inquiry. Kirkhart's theory (this volume) of integrated influence is then used to analyze the utility of this needs assessment. Finally, suggestions are made about how evaluation use can continue to evolve in educational contexts.

Evaluation Use in School-University Partnerships

In education, school-university partnerships are typically established to facilitate the achievement of goals that require resources beyond the limits of individuals and their organizations. Joint initiatives are designed to sponsor *services, products,* and *processes* that would normally remain outside the capacity of either partner. Evaluation has a history of being useful in the realization of goals in all three of these partnership contexts. Some examples will help illustrate this point.

Evaluation in Service-Focused Partnerships. When the motivation for pooling resources is to address the needs of a mutual client, the partnership will have a service-focused dimension. Universities and schools typically establish partnerships around the education of new teachers. Colleges of education would be the first to argue the need for teacher candidates to experience a significant portion of their professional education in schools and classrooms (Upitis, 2000). Schools are open to this kind of partnership because they value the contributions that preservice teachers make to their communities. In a partnership of this kind, partners must see their contributions as equitable. It is essential that the services offered by the university counterbalance, to some extent, the supervisory and administrative responsibilities that are inherent in the on-site mentoring relationships.

Teacher education at Queen's University, Kingston, Canada, is typical in that it relies on the willing involvement of schools and teachers for its field-based component. Systematic evaluation of this program element between 1997 and 1999 was initiated by the university, not only to discover more about the workings of the practicum (Lock, Munby, Hutchinson, and Whitehead, 2000) but also to extend understandings of what it meant to develop, support, and sustain a productive school-university partnership around the development of teachers. In the latter case, the evaluation was about "two cultures meeting over a common interest" (Martin, Munby, and Hutchinson, 2000, p. 280) and highlighted the contributions of both partners in the ongoing development of competent professional educators (Shulha and Munby, 2000).

Evaluation in Product-Focused Partnerships. School-university partnerships have also proven to be useful when teachers or their schools are in need of a particular product. Program evaluations, innovative curricula, and professional development packages are all typical products of university-school partnerships. When the desired product is an evaluation report, collaborative stakeholder designs for the evaluation are common. University-based evaluators and school personnel establish the roles and goals that allow them to work cooperatively although intermittently. The partnership is most active at the beginning as questions are clarified, throughout the data collection while stakeholders act as data sources, and near the end when the alliance helps make sense of emerging data. This approach invests authority in the evaluator to shape the interactions of the partnership and to optimize the adequacy, appropriateness, and trustworthiness of findings. Brandon (1998) supports the choice of stakeholder designs in contexts in which formal products are required. He argues that setting limits on how and when stakeholders are involved makes it more likely that adequate data will be collected on the constructs most relevant to that particular evaluation. Evaluations grounded in this type of partnership can still be versatile, providing schools with reports that are of instrumental, conceptual, and symbolic use (Leviton and Hughes, 1981).

Evaluation in Process-Focused Partnerships. The practice of establishing school-university partnerships to facilitate inquiry has a long history in education. When Kurt Lewin coined the phrase *action research* in 1944, a body of literature began to formalize around the practice. A significant analysis of the history, traditions, popularity, and complexities of action research is provided by King and Lonnquist (1992). The emergence of evaluation as a vehicle for joint inquiry grew out of evaluators' concerns about evaluation use. "Evaluators, frustrated by their interactions with resistant program personnel and little evidence that their efforts were serving any real purpose, began exploring and articulating means for increasing involvement and ownership of the evaluation process and findings" (Torres, Padilla, Stone, Butkus, Hook, Casey and Arens, 2000, p. 28).

In 1996, a survey of North American evaluators with membership in the American Evaluation Association's topical interest group Evaluation Use (n = 257) captured an apparent shift in evaluation practice. Although formative and improvement-focused evaluations remained predominant, evaluators reported attending more often to the learning needs of program personnel and their organizations. In many cases, responding evaluators expressed the belief that these considerations were at the center of the evaluation enterprise (Preskill and Caracelli, 1997). These findings confirm the increasing willingness of evaluators to work in more participatory, empowering, and developmental ways (see Cousins and Earl, 1992; Fetterman, Kaftarian, and Wandersman, 1996; Patton, 1997, for details on these approaches).

Common among these newer designs is the extensive participation of program people in the full range of evaluation activities (Cousins, Donahue, and Bloom, 1996). Participatory frameworks have made a significant contribution to the understanding of the potential of evaluation use. Frequent and intensive interactions between evaluators and practitioners have led to the in-depth examination of program contexts and the complex dilemmas that reside there. "As the acknowledged inter-relationships between evaluation and program context became more acute, so did interest in the potential to foster growth in the program community as a whole" (Shulha and Cousins, 1997, p. 199). Practitioners working with participatory evaluators have learned not only about the design and conduct of evaluations but also about how the inquiry process can support ongoing learning (Lafleur, 1995; Lee and Cousins, 1995).

Summary. Evaluation has a rich history of facilitating and supporting school-university partnerships in instrumental ways. The more recent learning-oriented evaluations have demonstrated their utility in partnerships in which the primary focus is to understand and improve the teaching, learning, and schooling processes. Practitioners in this type of partnership often acquire a deeper working knowledge of their professional context and a skill set that is applicable to future evaluative tasks. What remains unknown is how influential these learnings are for those not identified as primary participants in the partnership and how sustainable these new learnings are without the focus of an evaluation project to reinforce them.

Evaluative Inquiry and Professional Learning

Preskill and Torres (1999) make the case that evaluative inquiry structured within the workplace provides opportunities for organizational learning. In constructing the frameworks and tools to support this purpose, they make a useful distinction between evaluation and evaluative inquiry. Whereas an evaluation is usually an event that overlays regular work routines, "evaluative inquiry is integrated into the organization's work process and is performed primarily by organization members" (p. 184). In evaluation, start dates and report dates anchor a task-time line that provides structure to the inquiry. Movement along this line defines progress in the evaluation. "Evaluative inquiry for organizational learning is ongoing; it is not episodic. . . . It is both iterative and self-renewing" (p. 184–185). Depending on the purpose of the evaluation, the selection of stakeholders or participants will vary in role, number, and involvement. Evaluative inquiry "relies on the democratic process of asking questions and exploring individuals' values, beliefs, assumptions and knowledge through dialogue and reflection. It seeks to include a diversity of voices" (p. 185). Evaluation may or may not have practitioners examine their work lives in relation to the needs, values, or beliefs of others. It has no responsibility to contribute to a culture of inquiry. Evaluative inquiry must make these contributions. "Its processes and findings nourish the development of interpersonal and professional relationships, and strengthen organizational decision making" (p. 185).

Preskill and Torres admit that their aspirations for evaluative inquiry and for organizational learning are idealistic. For a school to restructure around the promises of evaluative inquiry, there would need to be irrefutable evidence that teaching, learning, and administering were significantly enhanced by the practice. This is not immediately forthcoming. Even if strong links between teacher and school effectiveness and ongoing, structured evaluative inquiry do become established, there is a risk that the complexity of the process will be minimized and the power of the process lost in a formula for "best practice." A more desirable option would be for teachers and administrators to discover the benefits of evaluative inquiry firsthand in the context of real work. School-university partnerships tailored around school-identified professional learning needs might turn out to be the ideal proving ground for evaluative inquiry. Fidelity to the process would then be based only on the degree to which educators were able to demonstrate interdependent, adequate, and creative use of information in addressing the challenges of teaching, learning, and schooling. What follows is the opening segment of a story that over four years featured the continual use of evaluative inquiry in support of both individual and organizational learning. This segment was chosen because it reveals how evaluative inquiry was introduced and how the resultant learning shaped the expectations for partnership.

Considering a School-University Professional Learning Partnership

In 1996, Martin Felton, the director of a large prekindergarten through grade-twelve international school in Colombia, South America (Colegio Bolívar), and Rena Upitis, the dean of a faculty of education (Queen's University at Kingston, Canada), in consultation with a small number of faculty from both sites, began to explore the viability of a formal learning partnership. The director was concerned that the school's investment in professional development activities for individual teachers was having little effect on the quality of teaching and learning at the school. As predicted by the literature, both administrators saw an opportunity to advance organizational goals through access to resources that were not readily available in-house. Bolívar would have access to tailored, on-site professional development, and Queen's faculty would work in a community of practice rich in research-and-development opportunities. In addition, Queen's University looked at this as an opportunity to explore the pragmatic and financial implications of making a long-term commitment to university-school learning partnerships.

The agreement in principle reached between the two administrators set the stage for negotiating a partnership, but it did not mandate one. Although minimal expectations for the investment of time at both sites and a plan for acquiring and distributing resources were agreed on, the appropriateness and utility of the partnership for teachers and academics were yet to be determined. It was significant, however, that enthusiasm for the partnership did exist at an administrative level. Much has been written about the ability of an organization's administration to promote, block, or stifle the change process (Burry, Alkin, and Ruskus, 1985; Cousins, 1996; Shulha and Wilson, 1995).

It was agreed that the fate of the partnership would rest ultimately in teachers' hands and that their decision should be anchored in the findings of a needs assessment. The responsibility for facilitating this inquiry was assigned to two university faculty members with backgrounds in program evaluation, Lyn Shulha and Robert Wilson.

In reflecting on this process some months later, it became apparent to the evaluators that a number of assumptions were implicit in their approach:

- Systematic evaluative inquiry generates information useful for decision making at both an individual and an organizational level.
- Participation in systematic evaluative inquiry builds capacity both in an individual and in an organization for future problem solving.
- Shared experiences do not necessarily result in shared meanings; shared meaning making between academics and practitioners is the foundation of new knowledge about professional practice.

- Teachers and researchers bring with them to the inquiry process complementary expertise: the researcher is conversant in theory, practice, and analysis as they play out in more general terms, and the practitioner is knowledgeable about the elements of context (school policies, structures, culture, and student characteristics) as these tend to shape local decision making.
- Successful professional development allows teachers and researchers to learn *from* as well as *about* practice (Shulha and Wilson, 1997).

These assumptions were derived from a number of fields of inquiry that supported the evaluators' ongoing work at the university. Other than program evaluation, these fields included collaborative research (for example, Bickel and Hattrup, 1995; Shulha and others, 1997; Ulichny and Schoener, 1996), cognitive development and structures of learning (for example, Benner, 1984; Biggs, 1982), student assessment (for example, Wilson, 1996), learning in organizations (for example, Argyris and Schön, 1996; Preskill, 1994), and knowledge utilization (Cousins and Shulha, 1997; Hargraves, 1996; Huberman, 1990). At the time, however, the focus was not on testing any particular relationship among these assumptions. Rather the challenge was to design a needs assessment that would be powerful enough to actively engage all of us in evaluative inquiry, prepare us for decision making, and leave us with new understandings about professional learning.

The Needs Assessment

Data for the needs assessment came from three sources. The primary source was a survey instrument, Building a Program of Professional Development. With input from both administrators, the evaluators were charged with the design of the survey. In taking on this task, their primary concern was that teachers be given the chance to express their own notions of optimal professional learning. One of the challenges for the evaluative inquiry would be to discover the consistency of these notions and to determine if a partnership could be shaped to reflect these ideas. The survey consisted of both selected response and open-ended questions and asked Colegio Bolívar teachers to consider what good teaching and learning looked like, what either facilitated or constrained them in their work, and what professional issues were most relevant to them at the time. The survey was distributed during the last month of school and collected on the last day before the summer break. The requirement that teachers turn in the survey before signing off for the summer ensured a 100 percent response rate from the 114 teachers.

For two days during the first week of the teachers' summer vacation, we (Shulha and Wilson) met with eighteen teachers who had volunteered to work with us in analyzing the survey and in making a recommendation about the desirability of the partnership. As evaluators, our tasks were to ensure the accurate and adequate analysis of the survey data to gain a better understanding of the needs of the teachers and their school and to make a recommendation about the desirability of the partnership to our university. In practice, we were all involved in sorting and analyzing data, making judgments about their meaning, summarizing findings, and preparing for the informal on-site report and the more formal technical report. In this regard, many of our behaviors were consistent with those of evaluators and primary users conducting practical participatory evaluations (Cousins, 1998).

Although the surveys were the primary data source for our tasks, a second data source was the ongoing conversation of the teachers in the work group. Their questions and comments as they proceeded with the assigned tasks provided important feedback about the quality of their learning and their commitment to the task. At times, these data came from break-out discussions and lunchtime conversations. These more informal interactions were significant because they provided additional "spaces" in which individuals could connect what they were learning about their colleagues and their school with their own emerging ideas of what a partnership might look like. Regular, formal debriefings of "where are we now?" made it possible to integrate discussion from both the formal and informal contexts into our ongoing work.

The third type of data that was integrated into the needs assessment process was observational. As evaluators, we were sensitive to the fact that Bolívar faculty would be observing our approach to learning. Their task, after all, was to decide whether a professional learning partnership with academics would be useful. We were conscious of presenting ourselves as good listeners. In the best of conditions, listening provides valuable information about the progress that individuals are making at integrating new ideas and skills. Our listening behaviors were challenged and refined over the course of the needs assessment as we become more comfortable with the pace and limitations of having participants working in two languages.

We also wanted to demonstrate our sensitivity to individual needs. Some of our work group were balancing outside responsibilities such as family obligations and summer school responsibilities. Although total commitment of all people at all times to a task is ideal, it is not always practical. Teachers watched as we found ways to optimize the contributions of individuals who were there and to integrate those who needed to move in and out of the process at various times. We attempted to make our time together enjoyable. Episodes of seriousness, intensity, and precision in thinking were followed by opportunities for lightheartedness, creativity, and risk taking.

While Bolívar faculty monitored one another and us, we also watched them. To ensure the accuracy and adequacy of our individual observations, time was set aside each day to review what each of us had observed and inferred about the teachers. There was consistency in our sense of their seriousness in learning about evaluative inquiry, their persistence while working in Spanish and English, their dedication to their students, their willingness to ask us and one another tough questions about what it would mean to commit to a partnership, and their general care and concern for one another and their school community.

The Findings and Their Use

At the end of our two-day process, the evaluators and school personnel had learned much about one another, about evaluative inquiry, and about the potential for a school-university learning partnership. From the survey, we were able to develop a description of the current state of teaching and learning at Bolívar. It was a description that would provide baseline data from which changes in behavior could be monitored. We also summarized the reported constraints to optimal teaching and learning. This summary included the role that individuals, organizational structures, and policies and procedures played in maintaining current conditions. Finally, a list of desired professional development activities was generated and prioritized.

Data from all sources also contributed to the proposed structure for learning: (a) A group of twenty-four to thirty teachers would volunteer to work with two academics around topics identified by the survey (for example, student assessment). (b) Although much of the work would be done individually and in small groups, activities involving the whole staff in the consideration of these topics would also be designed. (c) At least some of the mentoring between academics and teachers would occur in teachers' classrooms. (d) There would be two on-site work sessions per year, each lasting six days. These would be scheduled four months apart, with opportunities for distance learning in the interim. (e) Most important, teachers would structure much of their own learning around the topics that had been identified. Academics provide three kinds of support: relevant theory, adequate resources, and an approach to inquiry that would facilitate both individual and collective learning.

A third outcome of the needs assessment was a set of nine indicators that could be used to assess whether the partnership was working. These indicators, developed by the work group, made reference to changes in teacher, administrator, and student behavior as well as to changes in formal school policies and procedures. For example, indicator number one stated that "teachers should be able to provide evidence of what and how they have learned," and indicator six outlined the expectation that "there be consistent and integrated school policies based on the themes we have worked on" (Shulha and Wilson, 1997, p. 16).

Ultimately, the participants in the needs assessment work group used the authority invested in them to make an informed decision that an administratively proposed but teacher-designed school-university partnership was desirable. In making this decision, however, the work group felt compelled to put forward seven formal recommendations about how the partnership should play out. The three listed here demonstrate the power of evaluative inquiry to place individual learning into a broader context of school change.

Recommendation Two. That as often as is practical, participants in the modules come from a cross section of grade levels and that whatever the content focus of each module, the group explore the effects of grade level on teacher and student decision making.

Recommendation Three. That during each site visit, Queen's faculty provide opportunities for nonparticipants to be introduced to the purpose(s) of the module(s) and the central constructs to be examined during the learning process; and that upon completion of the module, participating teachers propose ways in which their learning can be extended to provide professional development for some or all of their colleagues.

Recommendation Four. That prior to each module, administrators and teacher participants meet to discuss ways in which administrators might become involved in the learning process and ways in which new learnings might become integrated into school policies and practices. (Shulha and Wilson, 1997)

Discussion

In the first chapter of this volume, Kirkhart proposes an integrated theory of evaluation influence. One way to test the utility of this theory is to see how well it accounts for the observed influence of evaluative inquiry in the launch of the Queen's-Bolívar learning partnership.

The question precipitating the needs assessment was whether teachers at Colegio Bolívar could find value in committing themselves to a university-school professional learning partnership. After being assured that their approach to the partnership was compatible with the values and intentions of their administration and the academics, teachers at Colegio Bolívar were eager to make this commitment. Visible, direct action was a consequence of the evaluative inquiry process. This suggests that the influence of the needs assessment was in part *results based.*

If we accept the premise that the capacity of an organization to learn is a function of how well individuals in the organization learn (Preskill and Torres, 1999; Robinson and Cousins, 1999), then a discussion of the influence of the needs assessment would be incomplete if it did not look at what teachers had learned along the way. These *process-based* influences were multidimensional. After examining teaching and learning practices across the school, teachers *thought* differently about the scope of their own work. Recommendations two and three discussed previously are evidence that through the needs assessment teachers began to imagine how their work might fit with that of others.

Teachers also *felt* strongly about how they wanted to work with one another, their administration, and their partners from the university. Various descriptions of the structures and processes that were to be adopted reflected this. Recommendation four cited earlier was an expression of teachers' interest in establishing working groups that included administration. The first formal module included a plan to open up classrooms to visits from colleagues and university partners. Small groups were to be structured around issues of mutual interest rather than around grade levels and instructional disciplines.

By the end of the needs assessment, it was apparent that our joint inquiry had fostered interdependence and a sense of anticipation for the first fall module. This is no doubt what Preskill and Torres (1999) are referring to when they describe evaluative inquiry as having the potential to be "self-renewing." Teachers, administrators, and evaluators were now "in relationship," and as time would attest, it was a relationship that would remain significant over the life of the partnership and beyond.

Finally, through evaluative inquiry teachers had reconceptualized their role in shaping the organization. The ability of the needs assessment to enhance teachers' *political* self-esteem came directly from the rigor and the transparency of the evaluative inquiry process itself. By the end of the process, there was a general confidence that the work group had learned meaningful information about the professional experiences and needs of their colleagues; understood the motivations of their administration and the university in proposing such a partnership; explored, in depth, the implications for themselves and their colleagues of committing their school to the partnership; determined the support that school administration and the university would need to provide to make the partnership viable; and identified policies, procedures, and behaviors that could be used as indicators that individuals and the school were benefiting from the partnership. In their own minds, there was no one who was in a better position to make a recommendation about this partnership for Colegio Bolívar than the needs assessment work group.

Moreover these understandings were now deeply connected to teachers' vision of the future. Teachers' ability to communicate their efforts and their findings first to the administrators and later to their colleagues is evidence of the depth of that understanding. The *immediate* use of evaluative inquiry was decision making, but *end-of-cycle* and *long-term* influences on professional learning were now being anticipated.

Many of the influences of evaluative inquiry were possible because of the willingness of teachers to learn. These influences, however, were not independent of the actions of the evaluators. Rather than simply facilitating the inquiry, we participated in it—that is, we used the evaluative inquiry process and the needs assessment that supported it to learn about ourselves, the Bolívar teachers, and their school. The significance of these emergent learnings is that they became folded into the inquiry as it progressed. Continual critique of our own behaviors and those of the work group helped us design more appropriate activities and more context-sensitive processes.

The idea of becoming a learning partner in evaluative inquiry will seem quite foreign to many in our profession. It is a role that challenges what we may have learned about being the disinterested facilitator of quality data collection, analysis, and judgment making. Greene (1997) argues that depth of involvement does not bias the quality of the process when it is undertaken to help participants examine the meaningfulness of their own program and its intentions and activities. "It is in the diversity of interests coming together to share the authority and responsibility for critique that the power to overcome obstructions is envisioned" (p. 33). The experience of the evaluators in the school-university partnership described in this chapter suggests that evaluative inquiry in a learning partnership is optimized when all of the participants, including the evaluators, are active in the learning.

It is accurate to say that the needs assessment facilitated but was not limited to results-based use. A decision was made to enter into a school-university professional learning partnership. Related process-based intentions were also evident. For a school director and a university dean who could not possibly influence the quality of the partnership at the level of individual interactions, the needs assessment was an ideal vehicle to make possible the transfer of power to those who would eventually shape the partnership process and its outcomes. For the teachers who volunteered to participate in the needs assessment, the process was an opportunity to test out the suitability of colleagues, administrators, and academics as potential learning partners. Finally, the evaluative inquiry enabled this group of teachers to declare, in a public way, their commitment to shaping the professional learning direction of the school.

Consistent with participatory evaluation designs, the evaluators intentionally structured the needs assessment so that participants would experience some growth in their ability to implement the elements of evaluative inquiry. The independence of the group by the end of the second day confirmed that participants did indeed feel confident in their new learnings. Having used the needs assessment to introduce evaluative inquiry, the evaluators had set the stage to make information-use skills a central element of the continuing partnership.

Kirkhart's integrated theory of influence (this volume) does provide a comprehensive framework for examining the utility of the evaluative inquiry process that launched the Queen's-Bolívar professional learning partnership. It has been particularly valuable to consider both results-based and process-based *sources of influence*. It may be erroneous to consider these outcomes as independent expressions of evaluation use. It is more likely that as administrators, academics, and teachers learned about the needs, interests, and values that were underpinning one another's professional practices and aspirations, it became easier to imagine both the partnership and the processes that would support it.

Conclusion

Partnerships are typically motivated by the need to pool resources in order to achieve increasingly complex local goals. School-university partnerships can contribute to each organization's capacity by augmenting the services, products, and processes that promote effective teaching, learning, schooling, and research. Evaluation, as a formalized activity, can support any combination of these partnership activities. Increasingly, partnerships are being struck around professional learning agendas. This trend is consistent with mounting evidence that traditional learning structures such as workshops and courses are limited in their ability to effect organizational change. The process that underpins this agenda is seldom conceptualized as evaluation. Yet evaluators who are willing to participate in these partnerships have a unique opportunity to establish the utility of systematic evaluative inquiry as an integrated feature of individual and organizational practice. Educators who become adept at information-use skills and dispositions are better able to work individually and collectively toward professional goals. Evaluators who are interested in engaging in learning-oriented evaluative inquiry and in teaching the skills of information use have much to offer the partnership process.

References

Argyris, C., and Schön, D. A. *Organizational Learning II: Theory, Method and Practice.* Reading, Mass.: Addison-Wesley, 1996.

Benner, P. E. *From Novice to Expert; Excellence and Power in Clinical Nursing Practice.* Menlo Park, California: Addison-Wesley, 1984.

Bickel, W. E., and Hattrup, R. A. "Teachers and Researchers in Collaboration: Reflections on the Process." *American Educational Research Journal,* 1995, *95*(32), 35–62.

Biggs, J. B. *Evaluating the Quality of Learning; The Solo Taxonomy Structure of the Observed Learning Outcome.* New York: Academic Press, 1982.

Brandon, P. R. "Stakeholder Participation for the Purpose of Helping Ensure Evaluation Validity: Bridging the Gap Between Collaborative and Non-Collaborative Evaluations." *American Journal of Evaluation,* 1998, *19*(3) 325–337.

Burry, J., Alkin, M., and Ruskus, J. "Organizing Evaluations for Use as a Management Tool." *Studies in Educational Evaluation,* 1985, *11*, 131–157.

Cousins, J. B. "Consequences of Researcher Involvement in Participatory Evaluation." *Studies in Educational Evaluation,* 1996, *22*(1), 3–27.

Cousins, J. B. "Stakeholder Issues in Practical Participatory Evaluation: An Integration of Research-Based Knowledge." Paper presented at the annual meeting of the American Evaluation Association, Chicago, November 1998.

Cousins, J. B., Donahue, J. J., and Bloom, G. A. "Collaborative Evaluation in North America: Evaluators' Self Reported Opinions, Practices and Consequences." *Evaluation Practice,* 1996, *17*(3) 207–226.

Cousins, J. B., and Earl, L. M. "The Case for Participatory Evaluation." *Educational Evaluation and Policy Analysis,* 1992, *14*(4), 397–418.

Cousins, J. B., and Shulha, L. M. "Recent Developments in Theory and Research on Evaluation Utilization." Paper presented at the annual meeting of the American Evaluation Association, Atlanta, Georgia, November 1997.

Fetterman, D. M., Kaftarian, S. J., and Wandersman, A. (eds.). *Empowerment Evaluation: Knowledge and Tools for Self-Assessment and Accountability.* Thousand Oaks, Calif.: Sage, 1996.

Greene, J. C. "Evaluation as Advocacy." *Evaluation Practice,* 1997, *18*(1) 25–36.

Hargraves, A. "Transforming Knowledge: Blurring the Boundaries Between Research, Policy, and Practice." *Educational Evaluation and Policy Analysis,* 1996, *18*(2) 105–122.

Huberman, M. "Linkage Between Researchers and Practitioners: A Qualitative Study." *American Educational Research Journal,* 1990, *27*(2), 363–391.

King, J. A. "Involving Practitioners in Evaluation Studies: How Viable Is Collaborative Evaluation in Schools?" In J. B. Cousins and L. M. Earl (eds.), *Participatory Evaluation in Education: Studies in Evaluation Use and Organizational Learning.* Bristol, Pa.: Falmer Press, 1995.

King, J. A., Lonnquist, M. P. "A Review of Writing an Action Research (1944-present)." Madison, Wisconsin: Office of Educational Research and Improvement (ERIC Document Reproduction Service No. ED 355-664).

Lafleur, C. "A Participatory Approach to District-Level Program Evaluation: The Dynamics of Internal Evaluation." In J. B. Cousins and L. M. Earl (eds.), *Participatory Evaluation in Education: Studies in Evaluation Use and Organizational Learning.* Bristol, Pa.: Falmer Press, 1995.

Lee, L. E., and Cousins, J. B. "Participation in Evaluation of Funded School Improvement: Effects and Supporting Conditions." In J. B. Cousins and L. M. Earl (eds.), *Participatory Evaluation in Education: Studies in Evaluation Use and Organizational Learning.* Bristol, Pa.: Falmer Press, 1995.

Leviton, L. C., and Hughes, E. F. X. "Research on the Utilization of Evaluations: A Review and Synthesis." *Evaluation Review,* 1981, *5*(4), 525–548.

Lock, C., Munby, H., Hutchinson, N. L., and Whitehead, L. "The Good and the Bad in a Learning Approach to Evaluation." In R. Upitis (ed.), *Who Will Teach? A Case Study of Teacher Education Reform.* San Francisco, Caddo Gap Press, 2000.

Martin, A. K., Munby, H., and Hutchinson, N. L. "Protests and Praise from the Field: Focus Groups and Predictive Validity." In R. Upitis (ed.), *Who Will Teach? A Case Study of Teacher Education Reform.* San Francisco: Caddo Gap Press, 2000.

Patton, M. Q. *Utilization-Focused Evaluation.* (3rd ed.) Thousand Oaks, Calif.: Sage, 1997.

Preskill, H. "Evaluation's Role in Facilitating Organizational Learning: A Model for Practice." *Evaluation and Program Planning,* 1994, *17*(3), 291–298.

Preskill, H., and Caracelli, V. J. "Current and Developing Conceptions of Use: Evaluation Use Topical Interest Group Survey Results." *Evaluation Practice,* 1997, *18*(3), 209–225.

Preskill, H., and Torres, R. T. *Evaluative Inquiry for Learning in Organizations.* Thousand Oaks, Calif.: Sage, 1999.

Robinson, T. T., and Cousins, J. B. "Internal Participatory Evaluation as an Organizational Learning System: A Longitudinal Case Study." Paper presented at the annual meeting of the American Evaluation Association, Orlando, Fla., Nov. 1999.

Schön, D. A. *Educating the Reflective Practitioner.* San Francisco: Jossey-Bass, 1987.

Shulha, L. M., and Cousins, J. B. "Evaluation Use: Theory, Research, and Practice Since 1986." *Evaluation Practice,* 1997, *18*(3) 195–208.

Shulha, L. M., and Munby, H. "Creating a Culture of Professional Growth." In R. Upitis (ed.), *Who Will Teach? A Case Study of Teacher Education Reform.* San Francisco: Caddo Gap Press, 2000.

Shulha, L. M., and Wilson, R. J. "Inviting Collaboration: Insights into Researcher-School Community Partnerships." In J. B. Cousins and L. M. Earl (eds.), *Participatory Evaluation in Education: Studies in Evaluation Use and Organizational Learning.* Bristol, Pa.: Falmer Press, 1995.

Shulha, L. M., and Wilson, R. J. "A Learning Partnership in Professional Development: Building a Better Bridge." Paper presented at the annual meeting of the Canadian Society for Studies in Education, St. John's, Newfoundland, June 1997.

Shulha, L. M., and others. "Collaboration in Research and Development." Paper presented at the annual meeting of the Canadian Society for Studies in Education, St. John's, Newfoundland, June 1997.

Squire, F. "Images of Teacher as Learner." In R. Upitis (ed.), *Who Will Teach? A Case Study of Teacher Education Reform*. San Francisco: Caddo Gap Press, 2000.

Torres, R. T., and others. "Dialogue and Reflection in a Collaborative Evaluation: Stakeholder and Evaluator Voices." In K. E. Ryan and L. DeStefano (eds.), *Evaluation as a Democratic Process: Promoting Inclusion, Dialogue, and Deliberation*. New Directions for Evaluation, no. 85. San Francisco: Jossey-Bass, 2000.

Ulichny, P., and Schoener, W. "Teacher-Researcher Collaboration from Two Perspectives." *Harvard Educational Review*, 1996, *66*(3), 496–524.

Upitis, R. (ed.). *Who Will Teach? A Case Study of Teacher Education Reform*. San Francisco: Caddo Gap Press, 2000.

Wilson, R. J. *Assessing Students in Classrooms and Schools*. Toronto: Allyn & Bacon, Canada, 1996.

LYN M. SHULHA is associate professor in evaluation, planning, and assessment, Faculty of Education, Queen's University at Kingston, Canada. She is an assistant editor of the American Journal of Evaluation.

4

A conception of evaluation as learning focuses attention on the critical inquiry cycle that incorporates use throughout the evaluation process.

Critical Inquiry and Use as Action

Gretchen B. Rossman, Sharon F. Rallis

The notion of evaluation as learning is not new. Over two decades ago, Lee Cronbach proposed just such a conceptualization. The first of his ninety-five theses on program evaluation states, "Program evaluation is a process by which society *learns* about itself" (Cronbach and Associates, 1980, p. 2, emphasis added). Learning is evident when it is applied and used by the program to "inform and improve the operations of the program" (p. 66). It is also evident when it "influence[s] social thought and action during the investigation or in the years immediately following" (p. 16). That evaluation should foster complex learning, applied and visible in action, is clear.

Cronbach and Associates (1980) also articulated, however, the recurring problem of use. Cronbach noted that "evaluation is not rendering the service it should" and that "commissioners of evaluation complain that the messages from evaluation are not useful, while evaluators complain that the messages are not used" (p. 3). If messages are neither useful nor used, learning is likely not occurring. How then can we conceptualize and enact evaluation in ways that foster learning and use? Cronbach is quite explicit, given this conceptualization, that the role of the evaluator is not solely that of external judge or assessor. His final thesis describes the evaluator as "an educator; his success is to be judged by *what others learn*" (p. 11, emphasis added).

In this chapter, we refocus and develop a constructivist view of evaluation as learning, arguing for a more complex and variegated understanding of use. We deepen and extend the work of Cronbach and of Weiss to elaborate the notion of evaluation serving an educative purpose. Consistent with this view, we suggest that the evaluator is a partner in the construction of knowledge and illustrate the critical inquiry process that fosters knowledge construction—that is, learning and concomitant use in evaluation contexts. In addition, we suggest that the evaluator's primary partner is the program's leadership. By leadership, we mean those who have formal organizational responsibility for the conduct of the program; this could be one or a number of people.

In the ideal world, all stakeholders would be partners in this construction of knowledge. However, organizational realities suggest that such full democratic participation is often difficult to achieve. As Weiss (1998) has commented, staff leave or change jobs, and seldom are all members of a program able or willing to participate. Even more important, however, is that program leadership is responsible for decision making regarding structural changes and resource allocation. Leadership can also provide continuity, vision, and authority. Consequently, we argue that leadership is a particularly appropriate partner because it provides a crucial leverage point for improving program function and outcomes. Together the evaluator and program leadership engage in a process of learning in which use is action.

Evaluation as Learning

When we cast evaluation as learning, what do we mean by *learning*? What do people in programs do when they are learning? And what are the implications of this for how we enact evaluation? This section argues that learning is a cyclical process that involves apprehending the social world, reflecting on those perceptions to achieve new insights, and taking action based on those insights. In addition, learning is both individually and socially constructed, and appreciation of the various qualities of the program and dialogue between evaluator and program leadership enhance learning (see also Preskill and Torres, this volume).

Fundamentally, learning is a process through which an individual transforms data into information that can be used for a variety of purposes. People gather data (sensory building blocks such as numbers, sounds, words, movements) as naturally as they breathe. They filter these data through their own unique experiences and existing understandings and make judgments about the meaning of the data. Patterns emerge, and the data coalesce into information. When a person uses the information in some way (to act, to decide, to form a new idea), the product is knowledge, and learning has occurred.

Clearly, learning is an active process that involves concrete experience, reflection, conceptualization, and experimentation (Kolb, 1984; Schön, 1983). A learner receives input (data) and immerses herself in the data; she reflects on the data, forming patterns and making meaning; insights emerge. She then applies her insights and tries out new ideas or actions. The cycle begins again as she receives input anew on the new activities. Active use of information, then, is inherent in the learning cycle, for what is application if it is not use? This cycle captures the essence of *praxis*—action with reflection. Articulated by Freire (1970) and others (see, especially, hooks, 1994;

Vella, 1994), praxis is the integrated process of taking action and reflecting on that action in a safe yet challenging environment. Reflection on action—thinking about it and trying to work it out—leads to insight and hence to the desire and will to take new action. Learning, then, is a consequence of reflection, action, and reflection on action.

The learning process is facilitated by social interactions that enhance opportunities for perspective taking, reflection, and alternative interpretations (Presidential Task Force in Education of the American Psychological Association, 1993). Thus learning occurs as the individual interacts with the environment. As Caine and Caine (1997) articulate it, "Our brain/minds change in response to their engagement with others—so much so that individuals must always be seen to be integral parts of larger social systems. Indeed, part of our identity depends on establishing community and finding ways to belong. Learning, therefore, is profoundly influenced by the nature of the social relationships within which people find themselves" (pp. 104–105). Interacting with others in complex social systems, individuals are not only learners but also teachers of their colleagues (The 21st Century Learning Initiative, 1998).

The concept of the social quality of learning is further developed by Fischer and Granott (1995), who explore the notion of *ensembles* as creating supportive environments for optimal learning. They argue for an understanding of learning that moves beyond the assumption of learner as solo actor. "People typically work collaboratively in small ensembles to learn and solve problems together, even though they can act and think without anyone else directly present" (p. 306). Echoing the positions of Caine and Caine and the 21st Century Learning Initiative, Fischer and Granott argue that people tend to operate in a fundamentally social way, working together in ensembles by sharing a task or problem with collaborating partners.[1] They argue that together ensemble members learn and develop in different ways by constructing knowledge and solutions. "This social nature of learning and development is so fundamental that it is embedded within human families and societies" (p. 306). The concept of ensembles has implications for work teams in organizational contexts (see Preskill and Torres, 1999, and this volume) and offers insight into fruitful relationships for learning in evaluation contexts.

Engaging in dialogue, an interactive and authentic "thinking-together," is one such fruitful relationship and serves as an effective facilitator of complex learning. Bohm (1990) differentiates dialogue from discussion. *Discussion* comes from the Latin *discutere,* meaning to "dash to pieces" or to "examine by argument" (Brown, 1993, p. 689), which evokes notions of percussion and concussion—striking or hitting. In contrast, *dialogue* comes from the Greek *dialogos,* meaning "conversation, discourse, valuable or constructive communication" (p. 661). Dialogue is generative; it moves beyond any single individual's understanding to produce new knowledge (Senge, 1990). Thus program leadership and evaluator engage in dialogue about what they are learning and move beyond either party's unitary understanding of the program.

Understanding evaluation as learning, as well as the concomitant use of evaluation-generated knowledge, suggests program growth and improvement. Program leadership and evaluator may engage in a process that in turn changes their perspectives: they learn from and with one another. Their dialogue guides decisions about data collection and analysis, which leads to richer understandings of program operations. This new understanding shapes decisions to support and improve the social value of the program. The better and more widely that the working of social programs is understood, the more rapidly policy will evolve and the more the programs will contribute to a better quality of life (Cronbach and Associates, 1980).

This perspective on evaluation as learning contrasts with the more instrumental problem-based approach, which is concerned for the most part with locating "problems"—the program's shortcomings to be fixed, the areas to be improved, what is not working well. The problem-driven approach examines program goals and looks for weaknesses in meeting those goals. This model assumes consensus on program goals and desired outcomes. The search is for instrumental solutions, for evidence to inform "correct" decisions. From the problem-based perspective, the evaluator assumes that both a problem and an appropriate solution exist. The evaluator is responsible for unearthing that problem and offering solutions (also known as recommendations). In these cases, use occurs when empirical evidence or conclusions help solve the problem (Weiss, 1978).

We suggest that the problem-based approach to evaluation is inherently limiting in that it deals with limited responses to given situations. In contrast, the learning approach seeks to raise questions, not address problems (for further discussion, see Preskill and Torres, 1999). "The function of thinking is not just solving an actual problem but discovering, envisaging, going deeper into questions" (Wertheimer, 1945, p. 123). The learning approach does not necessarily seek consensus; rather it actively searches for creative, divergent insights. "To raise new questions, new possibilities, to regard old questions from a new angle, requires creative imagination and marks real advance in science" (Einstein and Infeld, 1938, p. 92). The evaluation purpose of discovering "quality or qualities of the program" (Rallis and Rossman, 2000b), questioning what works and how it can work better, is consistent with an established approach to inquiry called *appreciative inquiry* (see Cooperrider and Srivastva, 1987; Hammond and Royal, 1998; see also the URLs http://www.appreciative-inquiry.org/ and http://www.serve.com/taos/appreciative.html).

Drawing on theories from action science and organizational development, appreciative inquiry has at its core a commitment to deep interrogation, to recasting what is working and how, and to focusing on strengths and opportunities. This approach does not focus on what is wrong; rather it focuses on what is working and seeks to nurture it. Hammond and Royal

(1998) describe appreciative inquiry as "appreciating and valuing the best of 'what is;' envisioning 'what might be;' dialoguing [about] 'what should be;' and innovating 'what will be'" (p. 12). This orientation to inquiry derives from different assumptions about society and change that shape concepts of use. These include, for example, the following:

• In every society, program, or group, something works.
• The act of asking questions of a program or group influences the program or group in some way.
• People have more confidence and willingness to change if they carry with them parts of the past, and the parts of the past to carry forward are those that are positive (Hammond, 1996).

These assumptions are consistent with the view that evaluation is learning and that learning is enhanced through collaborative dialogue that seeks to explicate merit and worth and explore possibilities. What is needed for the content of the dialogue is information that supports deep questioning and valuing rather than information calculated to point out the "correct" decision.

Historically, program evaluation sought to understand and appreciate quality. For example, program evaluation has been described as "the systematic investigation of the worth or merit of an object" (Joint Committee on Standards for Educational Evaluation, 1994, p. 3). However, the enacted practice of evaluation has evolved into a frequently resented, often feared activity that is necessary for program survival. We seem to have forgotten Cronbach and Associates' thesis (1980) that evaluation is "better used to understand events and processes for the sake of guiding future activities" than for "looking back in order to assign praise or blame" (p. 4).

We propose that evaluation explore the *quality* of a program—that is, its degree of excellence (Brown, 1993), and its *qualities*—that is, its characteristics and attributes (Rallis and Rossman, 2000b). Quality considers the program's intrinsic merit or goodness as well as its worth, or how it is valued by others. Evaluations that seek to discover and explicate the quality and qualities of programs can serve to make a practical difference in the program because detailed descriptions of qualities provide a basis for making informed judgments about merit or worth (see also Stake's responsive evaluation, 1991). Detailed descriptions can foster dialogue about what is and what could be.

Use as Action

If we view evaluation as learning and see learning as a socially constructed, appreciative process, then evaluation use becomes reconceptualized as continual and collective knowledge generation and application. From this perspective, use by the "commissioners of evaluation" (Cronbach and

Associates, 1980, p. 3) is not a concern because use is integral to the learning process: use has not been split off from the processes of evaluative inquiry. In addition, because the evaluator and program leadership are colearners in the evaluation work, evaluation use is not the sole responsibility of the evaluator. There is a collective commitment to integrating new learning into program operations and outcomes. Program leadership, then, is at least as responsible as the evaluator for the discovery and use of information for program improvement. As Weiss notes, "The many failures of evaluation utilization cannot all be laid at the door of the evaluator and her inadequacies as researcher, communicator, or collaborator. The potential audiences for evaluation should be on their feet searching for good information and demanding the best possible data" (1998, p. 274).

Application of learning—use—may be expressed in various forms. Traditionally, evaluation information was intended to be used instrumentally: the information is applied to specific problems, offering solutions or recommendations. In the past two decades, enlightenment use has been recognized as a common outcome of evaluation studies: the information contributes to general knowledge, enhances understanding, or offers heuristic insight. Evaluation results may also serve symbolic purposes, suggesting new ways to represent phenomena or crystallizing beliefs and values. Finally, evaluation information may serve emancipatory purposes by offering ways to act that transform structures and practices for the better (see Rossman and Rallis, 1998, and Kirkhart, this volume, for frameworks of evaluation use).

But recall Cronbach's assertion, cited previously, that "the intent of evaluation is to influence social thought and action *during the investigation*" (Cronbach and Associates, 1980, p. 16, emphasis added). It is therefore not just the outcomes or results of information generated by evaluation that influence. Participation in an inquiry process that enhances learning is, by our definition, use (see also Patton, 1997). Collaborative evaluation and participatory evaluation have become accepted approaches to bringing the practitioner into the evaluation decision-making process and to fostering use of results (see, for example, Cousins and Earl, 1995). Weiss (1998), however, notes that although stakeholder involvement encourages stakeholder use, outside conditions often interfere with intended use. Empowerment evaluation (Fetterman, Kaftarian, and Wandersman, 1996) and action research (Stringer, 1999) encourage practitioners to undertake their own studies of their own programs, but again Weiss (1998) cautions against "slipshod" (p. 273) data collection and analysis. Evaluation that holds as central the goal of learning and facilitates critical inquiry may lessen these problems because it alters the power structure implicit in the traditional evaluator–program leader relationship. Evaluation functions as part of the program; use is an intrinsic activity.

Developments over the past decades suggest that program leadership and participants have been split off from the evaluative function. For example, the huge growth in the evaluation industry over the past thirty years (see Caracelli, this volume), driven in large part by the role of the federal government in requiring external evaluation of its programs, can be seen as marginalizing evaluation from the program and vesting those outside the program with responsibility and authority for its conduct. Similarly, the residue of positivist science's demand for objectivity and neutrality requires external assessment of program merit and worth. As a result, many program leaders believe that evaluation is someone else's domain; they should not tread there or risk being accused of bias or self-interested analysis. Furthermore because evaluation is not construed as part and parcel of the *everyday work*, there somehow is no time to accomplish it. We argue that evaluation needs to be reembedded into the responsibilities and functions of program leadership. We recognize that ideally multiple stakeholder groups should participate in evaluation; given the realities of program operations, however, engaging the participation of leadership is crucial (for elaboration, see Preskill and Torres, 1999). This may well be accomplished by conceptualizing evaluation as learning and building program leadership's capacity to conduct and support critical inquiry. Evaluators and program leaders who collaborate to discover new understandings that lead to program improvement engage in this process of critical inquiry.

Critical Inquiry

The learning process that we have described relies on a critical inquiry cycle, the foundation of knowledge generation. The process itself is a cycle of questioning, based on empirical data. Critical inquiry is an open process in which participants reflect on data and critique their analyses and interpretations of those data in light of substantive questions about the program. The process probes deep assumptions about program theory (Bickman, 1990; Chen, 1990) and implicit understandings of the relationship between program activities and outcomes. Social interaction enhances the process as dialogue. One powerful form of critical inquiry occurs when evaluators and program leaders engage in dialogue with one another, asking epistemological questions: What do we know about the program? What do we need to know? How will we learn it? What do we do with this knowledge?

The cycle begins with accepting the responsibility for the program and what happens or does not happen because the program is in place. This activity establishes ownership of the program: What are we choosing to do with our resources? What do we hope will happen because of this choice? How will participation in or implementation of this program help us achieve this vision? What will success look like? How will we know? The dialogue explores criteria for judging the quality of the program; it explicates the framework for judging the program's merit or worth. What do we value about the program?

Next, the cycle identifies a focus for the inquiry: What do we really want to know about this program? Do we have intriguing puzzles or troubling issues that we want or need to address? Is something happening that pleases us or bothers us? What do we do well already, and how do we know this? What do we do less well, and how do we know? The questions identified at this point will guide data collection as well as the meaning-making of the data.

The evaluator and program leaders are now ready to collect data to inform their questions. Some of the data already exist; some will come from new sources. They ask, What form will the data and evidence take? Where can we find it? How do we collect it? How will we organize it so that we can make sense of it? What values will the data represent? What data are missing? Whose voices are not present?

The next activity in the cycle is intense. The evaluator and program leaders conduct mindful analyses of the data in light of their articulated values, and they interpret the information in light of the program's purposes. In short, they question the data and assign meaning to them. Guided by the focus questions, they group the data, noting patterns and rules, articulating relationships, and categorizing. They are alert for unexpected outcomes and surprises. Here the dialogue serves to clarify, to correlate, and to judge. Who actually participates? What do program participants report is actually happening? What are they doing? Who is benefiting? According to whom? Is this program activity related to another? Did this activity influence this result? What is working and why? Are the activities congruent with our values?

The dialogue naturally shifts to action and change, to application and use. The shift is epistemological, moving from *knowing through talking* toward *knowing through action*. Up to this point, the dialogue has been symbolic or communicative, establishing new rules. According to Habermas (1979), social evolution depends on two principal activities through which humans shape the world and themselves: instrumental action satisfies material wants; symbolic and communicative action facilitates social integration. Institutional rules are developed through communicative action; they set the context through which instrumental action takes place. The dialectical interplay of these two forms is critical inquiry, and it yields social evolution (Bredo and Feinberg, 1982). These new rules set a new social context for instrumental action, so the dialogue moves to explore modifications or changes in the program: What practices should continue, and how can we strengthen them? What practices do we need to change? What supports and resources do we need to improve or alter our practices? The success or shortcomings of past practices have meaningful consequences. Based on the learnings from the first, more symbolic and communicative, phase of the dialogue, program leaders make decisions that will make a difference in future practices. And then the inquiry cycle begins anew. The evaluator and program leadership ask how they will learn about the new or modified program.

Illustrative Dialogues

The following dialogues from our work facilitating evaluation of inclusion efforts in schools illustrate the cycle.[2] Contracted by a state department of education, we met with principals and the special education director of Wallasquamet, a district that had extraordinarily high numbers of children identified with disabilities assigned to self-contained classrooms. Although the state's goal was to promote more inclusive education, the district refused to accept that goal; they simply wanted the state off their backs because they felt their programs were fine. Our first meeting deliberated on what an evaluation could do, the first stage in the inquiry cycle.

PAUL: You just don't understand our district. Nearly all the kids living here have major needs. It's pretty overwhelming if you look at it. We're doing the best we can. I mean, it's a wonder we don't have more kids in self-contained! And now the department is on our backs.

SHARON: What exactly do the kids need? Can you define those needs? It sounds like you all face more than ordinary demands.

TERESA: Well, kids in my school come from some pretty challenging backgrounds. A lot are "newcomers," you know, immigrants, refugees, and migrants, so their first problem is learning English. We can't just plop them into regular classrooms, because they are so far below grade level.

DONNA (special education director): I think I need to clarify that. It's not that all newcomers are put in special ed. We have separate ESL classes they go into.

GRETCHEN: And do they stay in those classes for the whole year?

DONNA: It depends. Sometimes we just don't have any room for them anywhere else. And then even when they are proficient enough to enter regular classes, many are still below grade level. You know, it just makes matters worse when the department comes down on us.

GRETCHEN: So your problems are not all in special ed? What are your other needs?

LILIA: A ton! In my school, a lot of kids are from foster homes, so they have moved a lot and missed a lot of school. That puts them below grade level, way below grade level. They need a *lot* of attention, far more than a regular classroom teacher can give.

PAUL: Let's not forget behavior. Because their home lives are so disrupted, these kids have trouble getting through a school day without some incident. Again, more attention.

GRETCHEN: You've just identified at least three issues beyond typical learning disabilities—language and cultural adjustment, mobility, behavior—behind the self-contained placement. Do you really believe that self-contained is the best way to deliver the services they need?

DONNA: We know the department wants more inclusion classes, but it just won't work here.

MIKE: Well, actually, I have four inclusion classes. They don't show up on the census because the special ed kids in those classes have self-contained IEPs. I think Silvia has the same thing in her school. It's not so bad, you know, not as bad as the department thinks.

SHARON: So the label "self-contained" does not necessarily mean traditional self-contained? Maybe we need to describe what you are actually doing. Right now, it sounds like a lot of things are happening, some good, some possibly not so good. You may be meeting some kids' needs quite well, and some others may be falling through the cracks. Let's ask, What do these service delivery structures look like? How are they serving students? How will we know if they are being served well?

SILVIA: I expected the same-old same-old thing from this meeting. We all want the best for the kids, but it is always, "do this, do that," with no consideration of what is. Now are you saying that you'll help us define what we have, so we can see what is working? I don't mind that.

PAUL: I might like that. I know some kids in Meadowlands are falling through, but keeping track is nearly impossible. Do you have any ideas?

Our next dialogue was about data collection, the second stage in the inquiry cycle. We identified multiple sources, including several that already existed. We proposed data collection from sources (such as parents and students) that had not been tapped before. The principals recognized that one stakeholder who was not present was the department of education, so they asked what evidence the state would accept to understand the district's efforts. Eventually, descriptions were developed of the various special education service delivery programs in each school.

The group spent several sessions critiquing the descriptions. This is the crucial stage that moves beyond appreciation to evaluation. Participants passed judgment and probed some assumptions of program activities. The dialogue questioned the benefits in each structure: What is working? Why? What is not working? Why not? Who is benefiting? Which students? Which adults? At anyone else's expense? The following is an example.

SHARON: I was pretty impressed, Mike, with what you do, given how overcrowded you are in Hillside. You don't really have any self-contained classrooms. Identified kids are all receiving services in the inclusive classes. When one needs some extra attention, the certified special ed teacher in the room takes the child aside.

GRETCHEN: And sometimes the child is not even one with identified needs. So the regular ed kids benefit as well.

MIKE: Still, we do have that one boy who really disrupts things. You saw what happened. He really needs the traditional self-contained, but we don't have one to put him in. Can't we create more flexibility? What's keeping us from doing that?

SHARON: It does look like few opportunities exist for kids to move into anther program when their needs change. Children seem to get stuck in their initial assignment.

SILVIA: I see that some of my self-contained kids are ready to move into inclusion classes, but I only have classes where kids are integrated for things like gym and art. That won't do. We need access to a real continuum of services for kids.

GRETCHEN: I wonder if some alternative approach could work, some way to create the flexibility you need.

MIKE: Hillside is not that far from you, Silvia. Could we cluster or something like that? Maybe work out some kind of exchange.

And so change begins in the schools, the final stage before the cycle starts again. These excerpts from the evaluation process serve to illustrate how dialogue moved from exploration and critique to action. Together the evaluators and program leaders (principals and director) learned about the programs they offered and took action to improve service delivery. Their critical inquiry process also reminded them that they had overlooked several voices and reminded them of the imperfection of any plan, so they scheduled times to continue their dialogue and discussed ways to make their inquiry ongoing.

The use of the cycle by evaluators and program leaders generates knowledge. What makes the cycle critical is the application of information for improving the human condition. Action—use—is integral throughout the cycle; the dialogue produces knowledge in the context of application. The imperative for use is present from the beginning. "Knowledge is always produced under an aspect of continuous negotiation and it will not be produced until and unless the interests of the various actors are included" (Gibbons and others, 1994, p. 4). The process itself, then, is use. Rather than construing use as something that happens later or only in an intentional way, we argue that use is inherent in the inquiry process itself. The critical inquiry is social change.

The critical perspective reflects a shift from an emphasis on the economic and political features of social life toward an emphasis on the cultural and ideological features. Knowledge is seen in the context of its contribution to social evolution, specifically in terms of progressive material and symbolic emancipation (Bredo and Feinberg, 1982). Critical inquiry cannot focus only on instrumental action; it pushes communicative action. Critical inquiry, then, starts with action and results in action.

Social evolution, from the critical inquiry perspective, means forward change. Derived from nuclear physics, as in critical mass, and similar to Piaget's notion of the organic process of disequilibration, the critical inquiry process amasses data from the empirical world and engages in ongoing analysis of these data. Analysis results in the reorganization of categories and thus in emergent, new meanings. Partners move from a false stability (understanding) through disequilibrium to a more grounded state (knowledge). The new understandings produce action, which in turn serves as input for the next cycle.

Action emerges from the exploration and consideration of alternatives, grounded in a social justice framework. Critical questions seek to discover and achieve a more just program. They involve issues of power; and race, class, and gender are crucial for understanding experience. The process is visible, authored by a raced, gendered, classed, and politically oriented individual. The voices of silenced and oppressed participants are recognized and heard. Typical social justice questions ask, Who is controlling choices and opportunities? Whose interests are or are not being served?

Evaluator as Partner and Coproducer of Knowledge

The knowledge production of ongoing critical inquiry takes the burden of use off the evaluator's shoulders. It becomes a joint responsibility of both the evaluator and program leadership (for a contrasting position, see Kirkhart, this volume). For evaluation to be a genuine learning experience for program improvement, "Both evaluators and [program leaders] have to bring something to the table, too, their own covered dish to the collective party. Evaluators have to bring not only their research skills but their responsiveness to practitioners' questions and perspectives and their communication ability. Practitioners have to provide their first-hand awareness of the issues involved and—above all—the will and determination to change what is wrong" (Weiss, 1998, p. 273).

The evaluator's role, then, is as partner and coproducer of knowledge. The critical inquiry process is a shared heuristic, a discovery process. The partnership encourages dialogue, discovery, analysis for change, and small-scale experimentation. The evaluator serves as a teacher, a resource, a facilitator throughout the cycle, becoming an "old friend" (Rallis, 1988). Like a truly effective teacher, the evaluator offers a zone of proximal development (Vygotsky, 1978) that reveals alternative perspectives and possibilities. In the past, we have labeled this role the *critical friend* (Rallis and Rossman, 2000a, 2000b). The partners explore critical—that is, essential—questions, those that explore the heart of the issue and recognize the tentative and speculative nature of any answer. The critical friendship coalesces around a common purpose, evaluating and improving the program. Both partners are essential to questioning assumptions, collecting data, making meaning, generating alternatives, and finally, to using information to foster more equitable and socially just programs.

Notes

1. The 21st Century Learning Initiative was established in 1995 to "make sense of research on learning and learning processes that were fragmented in many different disciplines, and embedded in many different universities, research institutions and businesses around the world. The 21st Century Learning Initiative's essential purpose is to facilitate the emergence of new approaches to learning that draw upon a range of insights into the human brain, the functioning of human societies, and learning as a self-organizing activity. We believe this will release human potential in ways that nurture and form local democratic communities worldwide, and will help reclaim and sustain a world supportive of human endeavor" (21st Century Learning Initiative, 2000).

2. Our intent is not to provide a how-to manual for conducting critical inquiry dialogue. We recognize the challenges and requisite preconditions (see Greene, 2000, for a discussion and illustration). In the example we provide here, we note that we have worked in this setting long before this particular issue surfaced.

References

Bickman, L. (ed.). *New Directions for Evaluation: Advancements in Program Theory.* New Directions for Program Evaluation, no. 47. San Francisco: Jossey-Bass, 1990.

Bohm, D. *On Dialogue.* Ojai, California: David Bohm Seminars, 1990.

Bredo, E., and Feinberg, W. *The Critical Approach to Social and Educational Research: Knowledge and Values in Social Educational Research.* Philadelphia: Temple University Press, 1982.

Brown, L. (ed.). *The New Shorter Oxford English Dictionary.* Vols. 1 and 2. Oxford, England: Clarendon, 1993.

Caine, R. N., and Caine, G. *Education on the Edge of Possibility.* Alexandria, Va.: Association for Supervision and Curriculum Development, 1997.

Chen, H. T. *Theory-Driven Evaluations.* Thousand Oaks, Calif.: Sage, 1990.

Cooperrider, D. L., and Srivastva, S. "Appreciative Inquiry in Organizational Life." *Research in Organizational Change and Development,* 1987, *1,* 129–169.

Cousins, J. B., and Earl, L. M. "The Case for Participatory Evaluation: Theory, Research, Practice." In J. B. Cousins and L. M. Earl (eds.), *Participatory Evaluation in Education: Studies in Evaluation Use and Organizational Learning.* Bristol, Pa.: Falmer Press, 1995.

Cronbach, L. J., and Associates. *Toward Reform of Program Evaluation: Aims, Methods, and Institutional Arrangements.* San Francisco: Jossey-Bass, 1980.

Einstein, A., and Infeld, L. *The Evolution of Physics.* New York: Simon & Schuster, 1938.

Fetterman, D. M., Kaftarian, S. J., and Wandersman, A. (eds.). *Empowerment Evaluation: Knowledge and Tools for Self-Assessment and Accountability.* Thousand Oaks, Calif.: Sage, 1996.

Fischer, K. W., and Granott, N. "Beyond One Dimensional Change: Parallel, Concurrent, Socially Distributed Processes in Learning and Development." *Human Development,* 1995, *38,* 302–314.

Freire, P. *Pedagogy and the Opressed.* New York: Seabury, 1970.

Gibbons, M., and others. *The New Production of Knowledge: The Dynamic of Science and Research in Contemporary Societies.* Thousand Oaks, Calif.: Sage, 1994.

Greene, J. C. "Challenges in Practicing Deliberative Democratic Evaluation." In K. E. Ryan and L. DeStefano (eds.), *Evaluation as a Democratic Process: Promoting Inclusion, Dialogue, and Deliberation.* New Directions for Evaluation, no. 85. San Francisco: Jossey-Bass, 2000. Habermas, J. *Communication and the Evolution of Society.* Boston: Beacon Press, 1979.

Hammond, S. A. *The Thin Book of Appreciative Inquiry.* Plano, Tex.: Thin Book Company, 1996.

Hammond, S. A., and Royal, C. (eds.). *Lessons from the Field: Applying Appreciative Inquiry.* Plano, Tex.: Practical Press, 1998.

hooks, b. *Teaching to Transgress: Education as the Practice of Freedom.* New York: Routledge, 1994.

Joint Committee on Standards for Educational Evaluation. *The Program Evaluation Standards: How to Assess Evaluations of Educational Programs.* (2nd ed.) Thousand Oaks, Calif.: Sage, 1994.

Kolb, D. A. *Experiential Learning: Experience as the Source of Learning and Development.* Englewood Cliffs, N.J.: Prentice Hall, 1984.

Patton, M. Q. *Utilization-Focused Evaluation: The New Century Text.* (3rd ed.) Thousand Oaks, Calif.: Sage, 1997.

Presidential Task Force in Education of the American Psychological Association. *Learner-Centered Psychological Principles.* Denver, Colo.: Mid-Continent Regional Educational Laboratory, 1993.

Preskill, H., and Torres, R. T. *Evaluative Inquiry for Learning in Organizations.* Thousand Oaks, Calif.: Sage, 1999.

Rallis, S. F. "Evaluating an Old Friend: One Evaluator's View of the Challenging Role of Program Evaluator in Chapter 1." *Evaluation Practice,* 1988, *9*(2) pp. 25–30.

Rallis, S. F., and Rossman, G. B. "Dialogue for Learning: Evaluator as Critical Friend." In R. K. Hopson (ed.), *How and Why Language Matters in Evaluation.* New Directions for Evaluation, no. 86. San Francisco: Jossey-Bass, 2000a.

Rallis, S. F., and Rossman, G. B. "Communicating Quality and Qualities: The Role of the Evaluator as Critical Friend." In R. E. Stake (ed.), *Advances in Program Evaluation: Exploring the Discernment of Quality.* Greenwich, Conn.: JAI Press, 2000b.

Rossman, G. B., Rallis, S. F. *Learning in the Field: An Introduction to Qualitative Research.* Thousand Oaks, California: Sage, 1998.

Schön, D. *The Reflective Practitioner: How Professionals Think in Action.* New York: Basic Books, 1983.

Senge, P. *The Fifth Discipline: The Art and Practice of the Learning Organization.* New York: Doubleday, 1990.

Stake, R. E. "Retrospective on 'The Countenance of Educational Evaluation.'" In M. W. McLaughlin and D. C. Phillips (eds.), *Evaluation and Education: At Quarter Century.*

90th Yearbook of the National Society for the Study of Education. Chicago: University of Chicago Press, 1991.

21st Century Learning Initiative. "A Policy Paper: The Strategic and Resource Implications of a New Model of Learning." [http://www.21learn.org/publ/PP.pdf.]. Nov. 1998.

Stringer, E., T. *Action Research: A Handbook for Practitioners.* 2nd Editon. Thousand Oaks, California: Sage, 1999.

21st Century Learning Initiative. "The 21st Century Learning Initiative: Promoting a Vision, Knowledge, Experience and a Network." [http://www.21learn.org.]. June 2000.

Vella, J. *Learning to Listen, Learning to Teach: The Power of Dialogue in Educating Adults.* San Francisco: Jossey-Bass, 1994.

Vygotsky, L. S. *Mind in Society: The Development of Higher Psychological Processes.* Cambridge, Mass.: Harvard University Press, 1978.

Weiss, C. H. "Improving the Linkage Between Social Research and Public Policy." In L. E. Lynn (ed.), *Knowledge and Policy: The Uncertain Connection. Study Project on Social Research and Development.* Vol. 5. Washington, D.C.: National Academy of Sciences, 1978.

Weiss, C. H. "Improving the Use of Evaluations: Whose Job Is It Anyway? In A. J. Reynolds and H. J. Walberg (eds.), *Advances in Educational Productivity: Evaluation Research for Educational Productivity.* Vol. 7. Greenwich, Conn.: JAI Press, 1998.

Wertheimer, M. *Productive Thinking.* New York: HarperCollins, 1945.

GRETCHEN B. ROSSMAN *is professor of education at the University of Massachusetts, Amherst.*

SHARON F. RALLIS *is professor of education at the University of Connecticut.*

This chapter examines the stages of evaluation practice and use at a national multisite community service program with an internal evaluation department, reviews challenges to and organizational supports for use, and discusses Kirkhart's integrated theory of use at both the site and national levels. Finally, it summarizes lessons learned.

Perspectives on Evaluation Use and Demand by Users: The Case of City Year

Belle Brett, Lynnae Hill-Mead, Stephanie Wu

This chapter focuses on the development of evaluation practices and the consequent increase in both process and results use at a national not-for-profit organization, City Year. City Year provides an interesting case for examining use for several reasons. First, it has various levels of stakeholders. Second, because City Year introduced a centralized evaluation department as the organization was moving out of its start-up phase and into institutionalization, we can follow more closely the nuances of use and the ongoing efforts to encourage use over time. Third, City Year was conceived as an "action tank" for social change and has always valued learning from doing. Formalized evaluation activities have allowed it to develop its capacity to be a true learning organization as it has expanded (Kaser and Bourexis, 1998; Preskill and Torres, 1999). Finally, this case illustrates the many dimensions of use discussed by Kirkhart (Chapter One).

After providing an overview of City Year itself, this chapter discusses how City Year's relationship with evaluation evolved; how the internal evaluation department was able to capitalize and build on the ethos and structures of City Year to create systematic processes for assessment; how evaluation has been used at the site level, using the case of City Year Chicago; and how evaluation has been used at the national level. The chapter then discusses lessons that have been learned about enhancing evaluation use and influence. Because use in organizations takes time to develop, the emphasis here is on the stages and nature of the growth of use and the factors that have encouraged it.

NEW DIRECTIONS FOR EVALUATION, no. 88, Winter 2000   © Jossey-Bass

71

Overview of City Year

City Year is a national youth services organization with a complex and ambitious mission. It brings together a diverse group of young people, aged seventeen to twenty-four, for ten months of full-time community service, leadership development, and civic engagement. Started as a pilot program for fifty corps members in the summer of 1988, City Year, as of 1999, had more than a thousand first-year and second-year corps members in ten cities from coast to coast and one statewide cluster of towns and cities (Rhode Island). Each of these eleven locations is referred to as a *site*. City Year is a member of the AmeriCorps program network but continues to operate as its founders envisioned—as a public-private partnership, funded by corporations, foundations, and individuals, as well as by local, state, and federal government. Its service is multifocus, with an emphasis on service with or for children of all ages. City Year's vision is that one day the most common question an eighteen-year-old would be asked is, Where are you doing your service year?

Within each site, corps members are organized for the year into teams of different sizes, usually from six to twelve members. They devote substantial amounts of time to in-depth projects, such as delivering special curricula on HIV-AIDS and drug abuse prevention to middle schoolers, conducting after school and vacation programs, enriching school environments with special initiatives and tutoring, and leading young people in service. Teams are often led by second-year corps members, who are supervised by staff managers.

City Year sites vary in size from 60 to 250 corps members, with anywhere from six to more than twenty teams. An executive director, who has major responsibilities for the overall vision of the site, fundraising, and external relationships, heads up each site. All executive directors report to a national department, which advises them, coordinates conversations about future directions, and monitors progress toward key organizational goals. The national organization also houses several centralized departments, such as finance. Each site has a certain amount of autonomy, especially in relation to unique geographical needs and conditions, but City Year is interested in preserving some level of cohesion among the sites, even as it expands.

Part of the cohesion is maintained by City Year's strong set of core values and its culture. This culture is embodied in a distinctive uniform, which is worn both by corps members and staff across the country; its regular physical training routines; and its "power tools," or ways of doing things, which foster both order and a sense of being included. It is further represented by City Year's founding stories, folk tales, and quotations that reflect City Year's values of service, teamwork, individual contribution, and inclusivity, among others, and are used in all aspects of City Year life, from marketing to education of children. The unique culture of City Year not only provides it with an appealing identity but also creates a hook around which to develop aspects of the program and support structures, including evaluation.

History of Evaluation at City Year

This section reviews the history and evolution of the evaluation process at City Year.

Early History. City Year's relationship with evaluation began early in its history. Bain and Company, one of City Year's first sponsors, conducted an evaluation of the summer pilot program in 1988. In 1992, City Year hired someone to design tools and collect information for program improvement. In 1994, the first official year of AmeriCorps funding, City Year opened four new sites at once, and the need for evaluation became even stronger as AmeriCorps made specific requests for regular documentation. The organization contracted a consultant to develop a series of stakeholder surveys. City Year then sought and successfully obtained grant money to fund both an evaluation department and a training arm, called Academy, thereby setting in motion the relationship between evaluation and use. A professional director of evaluation was hired in January of 1996.

During the rest of 1995–1996, the new evaluation department, renamed Research and Systematic Learning (RASL) to emphasize the learning end of the loop, maintained and refined the survey process, added some new midyear instruments to help in making midcourse corrections, commissioned two qualitative studies on effective practices in service, and using a collaborative process, developed a pilot study for the Young Heroes program, City Year's special weekend service program for middle schoolers. RASL's first noticeable accomplishment occurred after the midyear survey process, when the department quickly turned data around in the form of short, but tailored, site reports. Sites thought that the department was working for them and not just for the national office.

After this initial period, RASL's work encompassed four overlapping stages that relate to use—building systems and creating a more learning-centered evaluation process, expanding site capacity for evaluation and sharing the expertise, changing the locus of ownership and heightening use, and developing strategies to address overarching questions about the processes and impact of the organization as a whole. We discuss each of these in the following sections.

Building Systems and Creating a More Learning-Centered Evaluation Process. RASL proposed a simple schema to help sites understand how information could be used to answer the questions most commonly asked about City Year by internal and external constituencies: What is getting done, what works, and what difference is being made? Using feedback from the sites, RASL began to develop tools and structures for the sites to collect data that could be used both by them and the national organization to answer these questions. These tools and structures included a quarterly, formalized reflection process (the *quarterly synthesis*), a storytelling component based on one of City Year's founding stories ("The Daily Starfish"), a database to track outputs of service (for example, number of children served in after school programs, number of murals painted), surveys to gauge stakeholder perceptions of program strengths and results, and instrumentation for assessing City Year's special programs. In creating its overall plan, RASL's aim was to be utilization focused (Patton, 1997), learning oriented (see Rossman and Rallis, and Preskill and Torres, this volume), participatory (Fetterman, 1996), and theory-driven (Chen, 1990; Weiss, 1998). Its intention was to align City Year's leadership development and *transformative service* goals and its needs for usable, persuasive data with a greater emphasis on the connection between activity and outcomes and on reflection leading to insights about areas for program improvement. RASL saw the heart of its early evaluation work as being team based, with corps members taking major responsibility.

RASL spent a considerable amount of time training and holding discussions with staff, not only about what could be learned from good documentation and evaluation but also about how, through the use of logic models, these processes could help them in designing their service (Connell and Kubisch, 1998; Weiss, 1998). Because of the size and geographical spread of City Year, RASL had to rely on a train-the-trainer model. The first full year with the new team-based evaluation and documentation responsibilities (1996–1997) had mixed results. The buy-in of sites varied, communication was sometimes difficult, and resistance occurred, especially from team leaders, who saw RASL expectations as extra work, and from corps members, who felt that the evaluation activities took time away from service. Instruments were viewed as add-ons from the national organization, and some sites did not even keep copies of their work to use as records of service.

However, in the spring of that year, City Year instituted a request for proposals process for service, and RASL suggested that as part of this process, program activities should be explicitly linked to intended outcomes. This crucial change in orientation laid an important organizational foundation for future RASL work and for City Year as a whole.

Expanding Site Capacity for Evaluation and Sharing the Expertise. RASL was much more visible at the 1997 summer training academy for staff than it had been at the previous year's academy. Its workshops, including one on use, were co-run with site staff and were well received, thus adding to RASL's credibility. In addition, RASL asked each site to choose from among its staff a RASL representative, who, among his or her many duties, would lead the site in evaluation activities. RASL held biweekly conference calls with these representatives and encouraged sharing of good ideas for training, implementation, use, and feedback on RASL instruments.

The RASL representative process, improved documentation from RASL, and a year's worth of successes and mistakes helped greatly in increasing information quality and site accountability. Several sites created a strong review process and did not send team-based information to RASL until it met their own stringent standards. By the end of the year, all sites understood how they could use the information at least to meet reporting needs. Teams commented that the quarterly synthesis process not only reminded them of their goals and helped them assess where they needed to improve but also gave them something to celebrate by helping them see all they had accomplished. At the end of the second year, only six teams out of seventy-nine responded that they did not feel that this process was useful to them.

Meanwhile some funders, including AmeriCorps, were increasingly exerting pressure on sites to show evidence of service impact. The multiple foci of service even within a site made it difficult to develop strong common tools to examine specific outcomes. In line with its emphasis on corps member learning, RASL created guidelines for teams to design and carry out their own small, yearly outcome studies, called the *project outcome studies*. As an incentive, RASL offered a small challenge grant that each site could match and use to hire a local area evaluation consultant to help them develop and implement these studies. More than half the sites took advantage of the challenge grant, although some began rather late in the year to collect any "pre" data for that year. Nevertheless on-site consultants were able to walk teams through a thinking process, even if teams were unable to complete their evaluation projects because of time constraints.

Changing the Locus of Ownership and Heightening Use. In fall 1998, RASL representatives, several of whom were in their third full year in this role, came together for a two-day conference to generate ideas for best practices in evaluation and evaluation use at City Year.

That same fall, the national program director collaborated with RASL in encouraging sites to complete project outcome studies, especially on service projects that might serve as models for the organization. In three sites, all teams completed Project Outcome studies. At City Year's end-of-year conference in Washington D.C., eight of the ten sites submitted posters, for a total of twenty-seven posters. The posters enabled staff and leadership to see what issues City Year as a whole was addressing in service and how these issues were presented through the eyes of its corps members. Although the scope of most of the service projects and the level of expertise of the teams about evaluation did not allow for highly sophisticated or rigorous studies, sites reported that the project outcome studies enhanced their understanding of RASL overall, gave them a better appreciation of an outcome orientation to service, provided a forum for forced reflection, and finally, allowed them to meet site objectives, such as obtaining more funding. For example, one site was able to show, through a sitewide Project Outcome study, that its teams had helped increase literacy among the schoolchildren with whom they worked. This evidence led to increased corporate funding for that site. In 1999–2000, RASL was able to obtain a line item for each site to cover the costs of a local evaluation consultant, and most sites took advantage of this opportunity.

Developing Strategies. At the same time that RASL was developing tools and methods for the sites, it also initiated regular targeted studies on topics of interest to City Year staff. Some of these are reviewed in more detail in the section on the national use of RASL. Another goal was to aggregate information from the sites to present a composite picture of City Year. In fact, anticipating a need during City Year's tenth anniversary year, RASL developed a database that would document key pieces of information from each of City Year's sites for each of the years it had been in existence. Prior to that time, this information was not available in one place. RASL was then able to produce appropriate charts and tables on the spot.

However, these composites could not answer a frequently asked question about City Year's graduates. To help meet that need, RASL designed and conducted a phone survey of a stratified random sample of alumni. Although limited funds were available for carrying out this study, it laid the groundwork for a much larger set of studies on City Year's processes and impact.

Before examining how the national organization has used RASL, we show, in the following section, how RASL's tools, processes, and results helped one site, City Year Chicago, strengthen its service and organizational capacity. We also examine the overall nature of use at the site level as framed by Kirkhart's theory of integrated use (see Chapter One).

Evaluation Use at the Site Level

City Year Chicago was established in 1994 as one of the early expansion sites. Implementing RASL tools and methods and using RASL data have helped highlight the particular challenges of being a service program in a large, spread-out city and have provoked conversations about areas for improvement.

During the first year of RASL's existence, the Chicago program director took RASL implementation seriously and was one of the first real site leaders in evaluation. She continued to serve as RASL representative over the next two years and trained her successor. The continuity in her role and her growing expertise in it helped establish Chicago as a strong site, first in carrying out RASL requirements and later in embracing RASL as critical to the site's operation. However, senior site leadership was also key in providing needed support and resources for RASL.

Chicago was one of several sites to match the challenge grant to fund a consultant to help guide the project outcome study process. In 1998–1999, all Chicago teams carried out such a project and produced posters for the national conference. A Chicago team won the poster contest, and the Chicago site was awarded the first Outstanding RASL award for overall achievements in implementation and use of RASL. City Year Chicago was able to produce evidence of change at several different levels and with different stakeholder groups because of their use of RASL methods. These areas included service project outcomes, service partner relationships, and management structure. We discuss each of these briefly.

Service Project Outcomes. Historically, City Year Chicago developed its service project goals based on limited information. Staff and corps members did not critically examine these goals during the year, and once the year was completed, they had no solid ways to gauge success.

The required reflection of the quarterly synthesis has reduced frustration as to why a project was not as successful as hoped for and has provided confirmation for those whose projects did indeed meet intended goals. By participating in a regular, structured, data-oriented process, corps members have developed a greater sense of ownership toward their projects and an increased belief in their ability to influence change. The process has also taught staff how to mentor corps members in setting achievable and measurable goals at the beginning of the year.

The addition of the Project Outcome studies enhanced opportunities for reflection. Site staff noted that the team that completed a study in 1997–1998 was the one that most effectively strengthened its service. In 1998–1999, the site required all teams to develop and carry out a Project Outcome study with the assistance of an external consultant, who created an evaluation curriculum and took each team through the process of identifying outcomes and appropriate measures, creating an evaluation plan, collecting and analyzing data, and writing up and presenting findings. Chicago began to incorporate its own local evaluation findings into weekly staff meetings. This broader audience provided teams with other viewpoints to help them make improvements in service and obtain feedback about the degree to which the service was meeting City Year's mission. Information from these various sources has ultimately had an impact on the type of service that City Year Chicago now provides.

Service Partner Relationships. In its first few years, City Year Chicago developed partnerships with service organizations based on what other sites were doing and what was familiar. Teams of corps members working on a specific project with the service partner generally managed this relationship.

Data from several sources prompted Chicago to consider new solutions for working with service partners. First, staff learned from service partner surveys that they needed to provide more leadership to teams as well as to inform service partners about City Year and the goals of a specific project. Second, from corps member surveys they found out that corps members did not feel empowered to make necessary changes. Finally, the team service *trackers* showed that corps members were not as frequently engaged in service activities that City Year would consider "transformative" as they were in activities that were important but oriented toward meeting short-term or immediate needs of an organization. These insights paved the way for greater interaction with service partners, including sharing evaluation findings and making these partners active participants in improving service.

Management Structure. The data, the resultant changes, and Chicago's growing need for the kind of information their RASL work was providing, coupled with their own performance appraisal process, also prompted shifts in the local management structure. Not only were staff given a much clearer set of expectations about carrying out RASL tasks, but the RASL representative became a member of upper management, indicating the importance that the site was placing on evaluation.

Challenges. As we have discussed, all the sites faced challenges as they attempted to implement and use RASL. Although most challenges were resolved with time and practice, a major and still ongoing issue is dealing with constant retraining because of yearly corps member turnover and frequent staff changes.

Summary of Factors That Encouraged Use at the Site Level. As we have noted, several organizational factors created a climate for carrying out and using evaluation at all levels:

- Commitment from the top to allocate time and resources to carry out and use RASL
- A committed representative, who was interested in RASL, participated in the RASL conference calls, developed innovative ways to make RASL work at his or her site, and trained and supervised team leaders
- An embracing culture that resulted in publicly shared findings and stories, corps member training in evaluation from the beginning, and a greater status given to tasks relating to evaluation
- Visible use of evaluation data to strengthen organizational processes

An Integrated Theory of Use at the Site Level. The case of City Year Chicago nicely demonstrates in action Kirkhart's integrated theory of use (Chapter One). Chicago first focused on the use of evaluation results, initially by the teams themselves to improve specific aspects of their service and later by staff and leadership to restructure their whole approach to designing service. In addition, after working with RASL instruments and methods for only two years, City Year Chicago incorporated evaluation processes into its daily work—setting attainable goals that were recognized and invested in by all its constituents, creating realistic mechanisms for attaining these goals, developing some of their own instruments, making site-based decisions based on data, and encouraging the growth of evaluation skills at all levels of the organization. Although RASL staff hoped that sites would gain insights about how they could carry out their work more effectively and that corps members might develop a deeper understanding of how they were making a difference, they did not anticipate the full range of process impacts, in part because each site carried out its RASL work in slightly different ways. Of course, some of these process-based uses, especially those around goal setting, were enhanced through additional support at the national leadership level.

Evaluation use at the site level also shows the time dimension referred to by Kirkhart. Some use was immediate, as when teams thought about their outcomes and prepared to carry out their project outcome studies or told stories about their service. Other use was at the end-of-cycle, particularly after a quarterly synthesis reflection or a review of survey findings. In contrast, Chicago's adjustments in its management structure were the result of accumulated data and insights over a longer period of time.

Evaluation Use at the National Level

Evaluation use at the national level of City Year shows a different kind of pattern, particularly as national staff are less involved in the day-to-day collection of data. This pattern has emphasized three kinds of uses—what Patton calls "conceptual use of findings," (p. 70) especially to test theories and generate lessons learned; instrumental use to inform larger-scale program and policy decision making; and persuasive use to make a case for national service as an effective strategy for improving democracy and communities (Patton, 1997). Nevertheless, as we shall show in our discussion, even the national organization benefited from process uses as well as from these more results-based uses of evaluation.

Stages of Evaluation Use. Evaluation use at City Year National has several overlapping stages. Some of these are now operating simultaneously.

Reflecting on the Program and Structures. During City Year's start-up years in Boston, staff sat down with one another twice a year in a retreat to talk about strengths and areas for improvement. Once a year, they invited service partners to a roundtable to discuss the performance of their City Year team and provide suggestions. The sudden growth from two sites to six sites within one year made this kind of personal assessment process less feasible, at least in terms of national policy.

Reacting to Externally Driven Evaluation Requests and Needs. As City Year simultaneously expanded and received AmeriCorps funding, its challenge was to meet the dual needs for site and national level documentation and evaluation. The creation of an internal evaluation department at this point greatly aided in collecting appropriate information that later on could also be used in funding requests, annual reports, and promotional literature.

Using Data to Make Program Adjustments. As RASL introduced its cross-site instruments, the national organization was able to make recommendations to strengthen its programs, thus demonstrating an instrumental use of results (Patton, 1997). For example, the director of the schools program implemented several small, but important, changes as a direct result of initial findings, and teacher satisfaction with the program greatly improved the following year. Other departments at City Year National were able to make similar adjustments.

Using Data to Create Program and Policy Changes. The shift to a deeper use of data at three levels of City Year—the sites, national management, and senior leadership—was stimulated by the work of a pro bono case management team that City Year's leaders engaged when they realized that their then seven-year-old model needed some changes if City Year was to reach its full potential. This team from Bain and Company, one of City Year's long-term corporate sponsors, was able to draw on RASL's growing store of stakeholder information and analyses, especially to show when service projects were most successful. The Bain and Company team structured its presentations to encourage dialogue among staff at the national level. In turn, City Year staff leaders replicated some of the discussion process at the site level. Thus a number of people at City Year became exposed to the value of data for making policy decisions and began to take RASL data more seriously.

For example, in 1997–1998, aggregated data from the quarterly syntheses showed that the teams' projected outcomes from service were not entirely in line with the goals that City Year wanted to emphasize. This finding, along with midyear stakeholder ratings suggesting that teams overall were not as strong as they could be, prompted renewed discussion about service focus.

The outcomes orientation originally posed by RASL has had a particularly significant impact on City Year's planning. In fact, desired service outcomes, rather than the specific activities or projects, are driving the development of new sites in New Hampshire and Washington D.C. and are influencing a host of factors from corps size and makeup to corporate sector engagement.

Data have driven other kinds of decisions. Survey findings showing that corps members' understanding of the connection between broader social issues and their own projects was related to the quality of their service experience paved the way for the development of a corps member service-learning curriculum to be used by all the sites.

Shaping the Research Agenda. After the first full year of RASL, Stephanie Wu, the national leader who oversaw both City Year academy and RASL and who had been with City Year since its beginning, took an active role in shaping RASL's upcoming research agenda, especially as it might inform service structures and recruitment and retention of corps members. In addition, as City Year continued to grow and faced the challenges of keeping a strong funding base independent of its federal funding, its leaders recognized that it needed to be able to answer big questions regarding its impact on its alumni, corporate partners, and the communities it served, as well as the efficacy of particular aspects of its model. Senior leadership became invested in securing special funding to explore these questions, and with RASL's help City Year received multiyear funding for such a study to take RASL into the next phase of its existence.

Integrating Evaluation into Daily Work. Senior leaders had regularly used a tracking tool to record each site's progress toward organizational goals, especially in relation to resource development and financial status, recruitment of corps members, and retention. *Results* was added to this mix in 1999. The department that oversees the sites now incorporates both response rates and service partner ratings from service partner semiannual surveys as two indicators of results. To meet National's expectations, sites need to develop and maintain strong relationships with service partners. This example of national leadership's integrating evaluation processes and results more thoroughly into its work contrasts with the all-too-common occurrence at many organizations of shelving findings once they have been used to address funding requirements (Sonnichsen, 1994).

Challenges. Despite many successes over the course of the development of evaluation use, several challenges and tensions emerged that prevented RASL findings from being used in a more consistent manner at the national level. Some of these pertain to expectations about and knowledge of evaluation, such as the speed of obtaining findings on long-term impact, the scope of data that can be collected, and occasional misinterpretations of results. Others concern the nature and culture of the organization, such as City Year's complex mission, which sometimes makes it difficult to disaggregate findings in a manner useful for creating change, and a culture that emphasizes action rather than reading detailed reports.

Summary of Organizational Factors That Encouraged Use. As with the individual sites, several organizational factors referred to in this section have helped increase use of evaluation processes and results at the national level:

- Influential stakeholders who understood the importance and potential of systematically collected data and who possessed the credibility to offer needed support
- External requests to provide sound data on processes and results
- An expanding and maturing organization that could no longer rely on a promising idea or informal methods for gathering information
- A culture that was seeking change, was open to new ways of doing things, and embraced feedback
- Opportunities to link evaluation with emerging initiatives and organizational priorities

An Integrated Theory of Use at the National Level. Supported by an internal evaluation department that can respond to needs, monitor implementation, and help interpret findings, use at City Year's national level illustrates all the complexity of Kirkhart's integrated theory of use (see Chapter One). Sources of influence are both results based and process based. Although the introduction of formal evaluation was intended to provide specific information to help strengthen the program as well as data to show evidence of impact (both results-based influences), the process-based influences have been broader, deeper, and possibly longer lasting than the results-based influences. For example, the shift toward outcomes-based thinking, introduced initially through the evaluation process, has had numerous ramifications on all aspects of City Year and its planning for the future as well as on young corps members' level of sophistication of understanding about their role in addressing larger social problems. Not all of this influence has been intentional, but most has been positive for the organization.

Process-based influences, such as thinking in terms of outcomes, have required a certain amount of repetition before they have become ingrained in the culture. In contrast, City Year has been quick to follow up on results-based data that directly suggested changes that needed to be made, especially on issues connected with service and service delivery.

At this stage of City Year's development, other than the office that oversees City Year's sites and program development, primary users have been middle managers, site staff, and corps members. As City Year moves into its next phase of evaluation, senior leadership is likely to become a major player in evaluation (Love, 1991).

Building Successful Evaluation Systems That Encourage Use

In the process of facing challenges to evaluation and evaluation use at the local and national levels and of capitalizing on organizational factors that encouraged use, we all learned some important lessons:

- Involve people at all levels, not just leadership.
- Start by showing how evaluation strategies can help address a critical issue.
- Increase interest in evaluation's potential by providing data that have a clear, immediate use.
- Respond in a timely fashion to and learn to anticipate data needs by staying informed and listening carefully.
- Obtain staff input into developing appropriate evaluation questions and assist them in framing answerable questions.
- Build, train, and support a cadre of self-selected experts within the organization to train and inspire others.
- Capitalize on organizational culture to minimize a view of evaluation as academic, inaccessible, and burdensome.
- Provide incentives, such as awards and financial assistance, and regular appreciation.
- Try to meet multiple organizational needs at one time.
- Present easy-to-understand findings focused on a small number of themes, and build discussion sessions around findings.

Conclusion

City Year staff and leaders are beginning to realize both the limitations and potential of being involved in evaluation, from the agenda-setting stage to the interpretation of findings. Establishing a culture of evaluation and evaluation use has been a gradual process that has taken root as more and more individuals found uses for data in their work and embraced the process that led them to the data. Stakeholders are accepting evaluation as a part of the program itself, not an add-on. Although everyone would like to see the "silver bullet"—that one finding that suggests it all works—City Year has come to appreciate other uses for evaluation. It has recognized that evaluation is a key capacity for an organization that wants to be both a learning organization and one that is "built to last."

References

Chen, H. T. *Theory-Driven Evaluations*. Thousand Oaks, Calif.: Sage, 1990.

Connell, J. P., Kubisch, A. C. "Applying a Theory of Change Approach to the Evaluation of Comprehensive Community Initiatives: Progress, Prospects, and Problems." In Fullbright-Anderson, K., Kubisch, A. C., Connell, J. P. (eds.). *New Approaches to Evaluating Community Initiatives, Volume 2: Theory, Measurement and Analysis*. Washington D.C.: The Aspen Institute, 1998.

Fetterman, D. M. "Empowerment Evaluation: An Introduction to Theory and Practice." In D. M. Fetterman, S. J. Kaftarian, and A. Wandersman (eds.), *Empowerment Evaluation: Knowledge and Tools for Self-Assessment and Accountability*. Thousand Oaks, Calif.: Sage, 1996.

Kaser, J. S., and Bourexis, P. S. "A Learning Organization's Relationship with Evaluation." Paper presented at the annual meeting of the American Evaluation Association, Chicago, November 1998.

Love, A. J. *Internal Evaluation: Building Organizations from Within*. Thousand Oaks, Calif.: Sage, 1991.

Patton, M. Q. *Utilization-Focused Evaluation*. (3rd ed.) Thousand Oaks, Calif.: Sage, 1997.

Preskill, H., and Torres, R. T. *Evaluative Inquiry for Learning in Organizations*. Thousand Oaks, Calif.: Sage, 1999.

Sonnichsen, R. C. "Evaluators as Change Agents." In J. S. Wholey, H. P. Hatry, and K. E. Newcomer (eds.), *Handbook of Practical Program Evaluation*. San Francisco: Jossey-Bass, 1994.

Weiss, C. H. *Evaluation: Methods for Studying Programs and Policies*. (2nd ed.) Englewood Cliffs, N.J.: Prentice Hall, 1998.

BELLE BRETT is the former director of research and systematic learning at City Year. She is now the principal consultant at Brett Consulting Group.

LYNNAE HILL-MEAD is director of recruitment and admissions at City Year Chicago.

STEPHANIE WU is vice president and director of the Office of the National Corps at City Year.

6

This chapter argues that pursuing use as the defining goal for evaluation can distort the allocation of evaluation resources and reduce the contributions of evaluation to broader social goals, such as social betterment.

Why Not Use?

Gary T. Henry

Why not use as the defining goal for evaluation? After all, evaluation is a practical field, and what could be more practical than use? Like the mighty Percheron, whose strong legs and back were replaced by a variety of machinery, without use evaluation will be let out to pasture and preserved only to provide perspective on the past. The use or utilization of evaluation has reached a vaunted place, supplying both a subject of study and a guiding purpose for evaluators. It is the latter sense, in which use is embraced as the Holy Grail of evaluation, that I address in this chapter. However, the study of use can slide into the same precipice when it ventures into prescription.

A series of studies in the 1970s exposed the Achilles' heel of policy and program evaluations—that the evaluations were not being used directly (Caplan, Morrison, and Stambaugh, 1975; Knorr, 1977; Patton and others, 1977; Weiss and Bucuvalas, 1977). Subsequently, these insights were formulated into numerous strategies and theories to shield evaluation's vulnerable heel (Bryk, 1983; Nachmias and Henry, 1979; Patton, 1978; Weiss, 1983). These prescriptions sought to turn weakness into strength, making use into the criterion by which the success of an evaluation would be defined. The most fully developed and articulated of these theories, first published in 1978 and significantly refined in later editions, became an influential, if not the *most* influential, theory of evaluation in the latter part of the century. "*Utilization-Focused Evaluation* begins with the premise that evaluations should be judged by their utility and actual use; therefore, evaluators should facilitate the evaluation process and design any evaluation with careful consideration of how everything that is done, *from beginning to end,* will affect use" (Patton, 1997, p. 20, emphasis in original).

Use crystallized the purpose for evaluation, and "intended use by intended users" (Patton, 1997, p. 20) became the mantra for a league of evaluators inspired by Michael Quinn Patton through his powerful and persuasive writing and through his extensive practice. Patton (1997) not only championed focusing on use but also, from the vantage point of a participant-observer, expanded evaluators' awareness of types of use, including process use and developmental use.

Use of evaluation is without question an important consideration if evaluation is to escape the plight of the Percheron, but should it be the defining goal? Should evaluators set out with the goal of use as the criterion by which they judge the success of their work? If not use, what? In this chapter, I begin by taking up the last question first and proposing an alternative goal for evaluation, the goal of social betterment. I then show that evaluation priorities are affected by the selection of one defining goal for evaluation over the other. I attempt to explain the way that the goal of utilization traps evaluators, a phenomenon that I call the *paradox of persuasion*. Persuasion is a specific form of use that is vital if evaluation is to lead to betterment, but if one begins an evaluation with the *goal* of persuasion, then the evaluation loses the credibility necessary to persuade. Finally, because the road to social betterment is long and arduous, I offer more proximate outcomes to assess the performance of evaluations.

Social Betterment

The distinction that I propose to make may at first seem superficial and strained: the goal of evaluation is not use; the goal is social betterment. Use then, although not the ultimate goal, is a means by which evaluation achieves social betterment. However, not all use automatically produces social betterment, and not all forms of social betterment can be achieved by pursuing use. Social betterment means improved social conditions, the reduction of social problems, or the alleviation of human distress (Henry and Julnes, 1998; Mark, Henry, and Julnes, forthcoming). For evaluation findings to contribute to social betterment, they must somehow be used.

But use is a means or process through which social betterment *can* occur. The evaluation enterprise is no less vulnerable to goal displacement than the interventions that evaluators study. As Caplan (1977) pointed out in his assessment of Head Start, the "original goals were far more broad based than allowed for by the scope of the measuring instruments. . . . evaluators lost sight of the original intent of the programs, and soon issues of race and intelligence replaced questions of emotional deprivation, sociological 'damage,' and educational achievement" (p. 191). Use, once injected as a goal or guidepost for planning an evaluation, can begin to take on a life of its own, rather than serving as a means to an end. In this way, use can become the defining goal of evaluation and in the process can displace and even obscure the broader purposes of social betterment, improving social conditions, and alleviating human distress and suffering. In their efforts to provide information that will get used, evaluators can lose sight of what information is needed to inform the discourse leading to social betterment. Although it is possible to make this distinction, is it, in practice, trivial? Hardly!

The goal of evaluation is to promote social betterment, albeit indirectly, by providing information to those charged with setting social policies, to those charged with carrying them out, to stakeholders, including service consumers, and to citizens. Whether social conditions actually improve depends on what is done with the information and on the quality of the findings (and perhaps on good fortune). Pursuing social betterment requires that three functions be performed—determining what constitutes the "common good," choosing a course of action leading to the common good, and adapting the chosen course of action to specific circumstances. Each function, discussed in the following sections, requires different information, which corresponds to different priorities for evaluation.

Determining the Common Good. More often than not, we define the common good by what it is not rather than by what it is. Take President Roosevelt's depression era rallying cry that "I see one-third of a nation ill-housed, ill-clad, ill-nourished." Although we could establish the principle that all members of society should be adequately fed, clothed, and sheltered, as a society we can reach consensus more readily about the imperative to confront the absence of these conditions than about the conditions that we expect to achieve. For instance, is someone adequately housed when sleeping in a shelter that is free from theft and violence? Or is it adequate to sleep over a heating vent when the individual involved chooses that over a shelter? Kendler (1999) notes, "Human cognitive ability is so flexible and creative that every conceivable moral principle generates opposition and counterprinciples" (p. 832). Democracies in which their members have the autonomy to express their views are uniquely suited to the generation of oppositional statements, and *value pluralism* is the inevitable result (Galston, 1999). Defining the common good is therefore usually a matter of defining a need or problem around which there is sufficient consensus that it is considered a social problem or, using Berlin's terminology, a human need (1998).

Evaluations can support and inform the determination of the common good by providing an empirical check on the claims of need and the extent or consequences of a social problem. In the field of public health, surveillance studies often supply information on changing patterns of illness and causes of death. Many states have developed performance measurement systems for public education that report on average levels of achievement and educational progress. Other evaluations may point up the fact that social problems are persisting in the face of existing social policies to reduce them or that some groups are not benefiting from the existing policies, thereby indicating an unmet need.

These types of evaluation are initiated both from inside and outside democratic institutions. In Georgia, for example, there are no fewer than four groups that compile and report on school performance. One report is done by the state agency that is responsible for funding and supporting public schools. Another is produced by an independent agency of the state and overseen by an appointed council. And both the state's largest newspaper and a conservative business-funded foundation offer their own school report cards. Foundations with social missions, such as the Annie E. Casey Foundation through the support of the state-by-state publication *Kids Count,* and policy advocate organizations, such as Mothers Against Drunk Driving, marshal evaluative information in an attempt to persuade journalists and policymakers that a specific social problem deserves a place on the policy agenda. Evaluations that empirically underscore social problems are those that show the ineffectiveness of current policies. Although evaluations that produce these types of findings are not planned to produce negative results, they often raise questions about the existing service routines and open the door for policy entrepreneurs to offer alternative policy solutions. For example, the well-known Fort Bragg study rigorously evaluated a highly touted "continuum-of-care" regime for providing mental health services and found little effect when compared with traditional methods for provision of services (Bickman, 1996). Thus the evaluation findings confronted the existing dogma about the efficiency and effectiveness of the continuum-of-care approach but did not provide any information that could guide the selection of an alternative regime that might improve the mental well-being of the service consumers.

Selecting a Course of Action. Evaluations can assist those in democratic institutions and ordinary citizens in assessing alternative courses of action that can be adopted as policies and programs. Rather than providing an empirical check on the claims about the social problem, these evaluations provide information on whether one course of action alleviates the problem better than another. For example, Gueron (1997) describes the welfare reform evaluations that tested the effectiveness of work requirements in direct comparison with existing programs. The reforms resulted in reduced welfare rolls, more employment, and higher wages when compared with the existing system. By providing a head-to-head comparison of competing alternatives, these evaluations contributed to the selection of reforms by Congress, the administration, and state legislatures. In a similar fashion, the original High/Scope evaluation pitted the very highly structured, child-centered model against more eclectic nursery school approaches (Weikhart and Schweinhart, 1997). The results show improved social outcomes for the High/Scope participants in comparison with those who attended the less structured program. The evaluation has been influential in establishing preschool programs for children throughout the United States. The relative success of states such as Kentucky, Texas, and North Carolina, which have implemented high-stakes accountability systems on the National Assessment of Educational Progress, has tipped the scales toward high-stakes accountability in many other states.

Even though evaluations that influence policy choices generally involve cooperation with government agencies, they are by no means always conducted or sponsored by them. Foundations can supply the resources to operate and rigorously evaluate pilot programs. The evidence of success or failure can be used to persuade policymakers about the efficacy of a pilot program as a policy solution. In addition, although they are not serving the overarching goal of betterment, private organizations often seek to evaluate policy and program options as well as training and products in head-to-head comparisons. Whether seeking information on how a new soft drink will stack up against a competitor or whether a marketing approach enhances a corporate bottom line, evaluations designed to provide information on the selection of one course of action or another are common to the worlds of business, government, and not-for-profits. What may differ is the frequency with which alternative courses are actually considered in the private sector relative to the public sector.

Even rigorous evaluations that directly compare one course of action with another support rather than supplant making the selection. One of the most important findings in the study of value pluralism is that it is impossible to yield a monotonic rating of the weights attached to various outcomes or effects across diverse stakeholders (Galston, 1999). Evaluations of this sort require a focus on some of the valued outcomes but inevitably leave out some process measures or outcomes that some citizens or stakeholders value. Moreover the evaluations are fallible and the extrapolation from one setting and time to another requires an inferential leap. Evaluation information should lead to better decisions by democratically authorized bodies. Rather than attempting to make these judgments, evaluators are on firmer ground by informing citizens and policymakers about the likely consequences of various courses of action (Kendler, 1999), thus providing a check on the excesses of political rhetoric.

Adapting the Course of Action. Evaluation can assess the strengths and weaknesses of the implementation of a chosen course of action and the organizational as well as situational barriers to implementing the action. What can we expect from a state-sponsored High/Scope preschool if the curriculum and instructional strategies are not understood or used by the teachers? Can we expect the benefits from welfare reform when the requirement to work is added but the resources and programs for finding jobs are not made available? Should a program that has been successful in lowering dropout rates for inner-city African American youth be modified for suburban Latinos and Latinas? What if the implementation of the treatment regime for hospitalized mental health service consumers results in rates for the use of restraints that are twice as high as those in similar states? Evaluations can raise these issues and supply important information for those responsible for making policies and programs work.

Evaluability assessments (Rutman, 1988; Wholey, 1994,), program templates (Scheirer, 1996), and logic models (Funnell, 2000) are all attempts to systematically provide feedback so as to adapt the chosen course of action or to adapt the organization responsible for administering the action in order to achieve better results.

Evaluation Priorities

To achieve social betterment, collectively we must decide what are the most pressing social problems, decide what actions should be taken to address them, and continue to refine the actions that are taken and reengineer the organizations that are charged with achieving the outcomes. However, rather than being neat and linear, all of these processes coexist and are more or less current in policy and administrative deliberations (Hilgartner and Bosk, 1988). Unfortunately, the resources for evaluation are limited, and not all issues can be evaluated simultaneously with a sufficient degree of rigor. There's the rub, the first spot where placing a priority on utilization versus social betterment begins to chafe. A clear focus on social betterment would use an assessment of the policy context to allocate evaluation resources (Mark, Henry, and Julnes, forthcoming). When competitors of the existing service delivery system arise, they would be evaluated so that information could be available to inform deliberations. As advocates press for governmental responses to needs that have not previously been addressed, the needs would be assessed. When a course of action has been firmly put into place and receives wide support, both improvement-oriented evaluations and those designed to detect omissions or other problems would be carried out.

However, with use as the goal, the perspective narrows. Rather than assessing the policy context, evaluators looking for the most immediate opportunities for use will be drawn to studies that focus on adapting programs or improving organizations. For over thirty years, since the term *incrementalism* was coined (Lindbloom, 1968), we have realized that small rather than abrupt changes characterize the policy environment. Some research shows that we have drifted even further toward incrementalism since then, in spite of recent trends toward divided governments (Jones, True, and Baumgartner, 1997). New definitions of social problems do emerge, but they are also relatively rare and seem to accrete rather than spring dramatically onto the public agenda (Glazer, 1994; Habermas, 1996; Nelson, 1984; Scarr, 1998). So neither new social problems nor new courses of action present frequent opportunities for evaluation to be directly useful. If we focus on use, either instrumental or developmental, resources will be concentrated on evaluations that support the third of the three functions required for social betterment, that is, adapting the course of action. The overconcentration on adapting or improving programs or organizations will occur simply due to the prevalence of these activities relative to the spare opportunities for the other two (documenting a social problem and selecting a course of action).

Because of the multiple interests and actors involved, no one manages the emergence of new problems on the public agenda, and no one has a monopoly on determining the next new policy alternative to be debated (Zhu, 1992). The judgments about which human needs make it onto the policy agenda and the deliberations through the media (Page, 1996), through elected bodies (Fishkin, 1995; Majone, 1989), and among the public (Monroe, 1998; Page and Shapiro, 1992; Stimson, 1998) will be ill informed if evaluation resources are not expended to inform deliberations about social problems and matching the problems with proposed solutions. Yet most of the time, the issues for which evaluation can most immediately be used are in adapting policies, programs, and the organizations that administer them. In a similar vein, the stakeholders who can sponsor or otherwise commit themselves to an evaluation are likely to have ongoing roles with existing policies and programs and to find the greatest utility in evaluation as an aid to management decisions.

Use as the defining goal is likely to distort the allocation of evaluation resources toward administrative or organizational issues and away from social conditions and policy issues. The most immediate opportunities for use steer the commitment of resources in this direction and give short shrift to the information needed to support the other types of deliberations. But is this merely a problem of providing balance along the temporal dimension of use (see Kirkhart, Chapter One)? In other words, can we maintain the goal of use if we do a better job of marketing the long-term, less frequent functions? Evidence from examining one type of use-oriented evaluation, evaluability assessments, strongly suggests that when the findings about organizational or program improvements are available, the interest in evaluation to support the other functions of betterment are not pursued (Rog, 1985). For example, once a program or organizational improvement–oriented evaluation has been conducted and the improvements have been proposed, short shrift will be given to assessing the program's merit or worth. Not only are other types of evaluation a tough sell on the basis of use, but directly pursuing use can compromise the evaluation, a situation that I refer to as the paradox of persuasion.

The Paradox of Persuasion

Persuasion is one way of labeling the somewhat inconsistently defined third category of use (Kirkhart, Chapter One; Shulha and Cousins, 1997). Unfortunately, persuasion as a type of use was sullied by its early connections with legitimation and symbolic use (Knorr, 1977). "Social scientists' data and arguments are used selectively and often distortingly to publicly support a decision that has been taken on different grounds or that simply represents an opinion the decisionmaker already holds" (pp. 171–172). Although Knorr did not find the evidence of the preponderance of this sort of use that ideologues had expected, persuasion seemed to be the seamy side of use relative to instrumental or enlightenment uses.

Majone (1989) admirably rescued persuasion from this connotation in a manner that is directly relevant to the pursuit of betterment through democratic institutions. "To decide, even to decide correctly, is never enough in politics. Decisions must be legitimated, accepted, and carried out. After the moment of choice comes the process of justification, explanation, and persuasion. Also, policymakers often act in accordance with pressures from external events or the force of personal convictions. In such cases arguments are needed *after* the decision is made to provide a conceptual basis for it, to increase assent, to discover new implications, and to anticipate or answer criticism" (p. 31). Majone, as Campbell (1982) presaged, recognized the deficiency of pursuing evaluation as a formal demonstration and shifted away from this moribund pursuit to that of evaluation as a tool for argumentation. The evidence from evaluation, by itself, does not conclusively demonstrate the choice that should be taken, but it provides justification and support for the existence of a problem or a course of action. Shulock (1999) creatively sought evidence of the persuasive use of professional evaluation and policy analysis. She recorded the number of citations from evaluations included in the reports filed by congressional committees after their deliberations concerning specific bills. She finds that members of Congress are most likely to use citations as the means for justifying and persuading others about their chosen course of action when committees were competing for jurisdiction and when public interest in the issue was high. So in the constant flow of potential problems and proposed solutions (Cohen, March, and Olsen, 1982; Kingdon, 1995), evidence from an evaluation enters into an existing soup of values, beliefs, preferences, and needs. The evaluation can be used to persuade members of the policy community and public, to justify a course of action, or to bulwark an argument. It cannot formally demonstrate or sufficiently determine what should be done (Majone, 1989).

Here is the point where the paradox of pursuing use for the purpose of persuasion becomes inescapable. When the evaluation is planned, designed, and executed to facilitate persuasion as the particular form of use, the evaluator must begin with the objective of producing persuasive evidence. The endeavor becomes not evaluation but "pseudo-evaluation," or an exercise of political advocacy, a well-recognized but roundly discredited approach to evaluation (Stufflebeam, forthcoming). Rather than providing a base of credible evidence that attempts to reduce the bias in selecting, collecting, analyzing, and reporting data, the evaluation picks and chooses ways to support the intended users' preferred policy positions if persuasion is the goal. Pursuing persuasive use can lead us away from social betterment if the information is revealed only when it justifies a preconceived course of action or supports the importance of a problem, which was already decided to be important. Evidence that indicates a program failed or that show that a problem may be less consequential than originally thought can be dropped as not supporting use, if use is the pursuit. Evaluators become advocates for a position, not advocates for raising the importance of information in public deliberations—in this case, information that has been as minimally biased as their skills and the study context permit.

Let me be clear about what I am and am not arguing on this point. I am arguing that if social betterment is the defining purpose for evaluation, then our efforts to identify and select criteria to judge program success, our efforts to collect evidence based on those criteria, and our reporting of that evidence are motivated and justified by the possibility of making things better. Evaluations that proceed with this as an ultimate goal can use principles such as complete disclosure of information and the requirement that information should "debunk bad ideas" within modern democracies (Hurley, 1989, p. 349). I am not arguing that use as a defining goal corrupts a particular evaluation or evaluator. Indeed, as I indicated at the beginning of this chapter, use can and has proven to be a sufficiently proximate surrogate for social betterment, and both lead in the same direction; however, they are not the same. With enlightened intended users and with evaluators who possess unswerving moral compasses, use is a reasonable goal. But as Madison informed us in *The Federalist Papers,* we do not have a government by angels. In situations with "unenlightened" intended users or with evaluators who are pressured to compromise the evidence, use can be served to the detriment of social betterment. Usually, social betterment or the larger social good supplies the criteria for distinguishing use from misuse. In these situations—at least when I have been in such situations—it is always the allegiance to betterment, the commitment to making things better for children or for service consumers, the commitment to democratic processes that provide guidance about what should be done. These are the arguments raised to defend openness and release of evidence that can be compelling to an identified user who is adamant about withholding certain information. The question of how society is best served, although there can be clear disagreement about the answer, pervades the dialogue for guiding every phase of an evaluation. The pursuit of use is secondary to this, although essential to the discussion as a means to the end.

If use, especially persuasive use, should not be the defining goal for an evaluation, how can we define immediate or proximate outcomes from an evaluation that can lead to the long-term goal of social betterment? For a clue to answering this question, I turn to the literature on agenda setting and the way that focusing events have been shown to influence opinions about what should be done.

Letting Go of Persuasion and Raising the Salience of Program Effects

Persuasion has been the focus of study for many fields and disciplines. After continued efforts to measure the impact of the media in terms of their ability to persuade the public regarding the issues of the day, Cohen (1963) summed up the situation this way, "The mass media may not be successful much of the time in telling people what to think, but the media are stunningly successful in telling their audience what to think about" (p. 16). A massive amount of evidence has been accumulated to document this assertion, beginning with McCombs and Shaw (1972) and resulting in hundreds of published research articles. This literature, which has been labeled as public agenda setting, finds strong support for the "link between issues as portrayed in mass media content and the issue priorities of the public" (Kosicki, 1993, p. 101). The media are effective in influencing what issues the public thinks are most important or are most concerned about. In raising the salience of certain issues, the media influence the standards by which the public evaluates the performance of the government or public officials, through a process known as *priming* (Ivengar, Peters, and Kinder, 1982; Krosnick and Brannon, 1993; Krosnick and Kinder, 1989).

The rather circuitous route by which the media influence public opinions may provide an analogy for how evaluations can foster persuasive use that leads to social betterment. Rather than pursuing persuasion directly, evaluations can be more effective by raising and documenting the effects of policies and programs for the public, program staff and administrators, and policymakers to consider. The effects can be processes, such as providing high-quality childcare, or outcomes, such as improving readiness for school. They can be intended objectives or side effects. The more proximate outcomes in the chain of events leading toward social betterment would include raising an issue from the evaluation findings for public deliberation. Or it could include providing an unbiased representation of the social problem or the ramifications of the policy that could stimulate "a shared understanding of the issue under discussion" (Majone, 1989, p. 6). Evaluations can contribute to the public understanding of an issue and influence the competition for framing the relevant issues of the day in very important ways by answering such questions as, Is the program working? How? For whom? In what circumstances? Providing a basis of facts that relate to valued effects or outcomes for public deliberations is no mean feat.

In this process, the criteria used in the evaluation become more relevant and more influential in the informal judgments about the policy or program. The public and stakeholders alike are primed to use the criteria in reaching judgments. Although they are primed to make judgments influenced by the information, the evaluator needs to be aware that the criteria used in any evaluation do not exhaust the criteria that some citizens and stakeholders will consider important for reaching a judgment. Value pluralism in modern democracies and the generation of counterprinciples for every principle being offered will thwart hubris in evaluators, policy entrepreneurs, or politicians. This tends to endorse the two-step process for the persuasive use of evaluation presented by Kendler, "The first step is to provide empirical evidence not contaminated by political goals. The second step is to avoid interpreting the results as directly justifying a particular social policy" (1999, p. 833).

Conclusion

Use has been evaluation's Holy Grail, the anointed purpose, which has motivated a legion of evaluators. By reacting to the issue of non-use and rendering this Achilles' heel of early evaluations less vulnerable, our work has escaped irrelevance. Programs have been improved and organizations have learned much from evaluations focused on utilization. Evaluation, especially in the sense of evaluation as a professional field of practice, has not suffered from lack of relevance but perhaps from too much focus on the short-run variety of use.

Clearly, modern democratic societies need information that supports the process of selecting one course of action over another and that assesses the extent and severity of social problems, even though the uses for this information are more infrequent and episodic rather than ongoing. This information is critical to our efforts to achieve social betterment and ameliorate social distress. However, questioning the assumption that the policy is the correct one for solving the problem (or even that the problem is significant) is not likely to occur to those participating as intended users, be they policy advocates or program administrators. If it does occur to them to question this assumption, they are likely to dismiss it because they lack the ability to influence these considerations and their "insider" biases. However, those in democratic institutions evidently sense the importance of these types of information because they call for it and their agents use it in developing and supporting their arguments (Shulock, 1999).

But information useful for persuasion in these institutions will not be forthcoming from evaluators if they decide to pursue providing persuasive information directly. Rather social betterment should be viewed as the ultimate purpose and raising the importance of policy effects in making policy judgments as a more immediate outcome for an evaluation. The results of these evaluations may achieve a circuitous route to persuasive use, by raising salience of issues and contributing to the stock of information available to influence judgments about the consequences of social policies. Being open in providing information, adding public disclosure through the traditional media and the Internet to the task of private disclosure through reports and briefings, and participating in the discourses of the relevant policy community on the social problem and its alternative solutions are potential roles through which evaluators can achieve relevance. These are the more proximate outcomes of evaluations that follow the route toward social betterment and the reliance on democracies, over the long haul, to debunk bad ideas when good information is made available. Relevance need not be sacrificed by replacing use with social betterment.

Pursuing use generally will lead to an overemphasis on organizational and program improvement–oriented evaluations. Instead the purposes of assessment of merit and worth, compliance and oversight, and knowledge development should receive their fair share of evaluation resources (Mark, Henry, and Julnes, forthcoming). Social betterment opens the field to a more deliberate selection of purposes, using the policy environment as a guidepost. Ultimately, the potential of evaluation is more likely to be realized if informing rather than influencing policies and programs is the criterion for success.

References

Berlin, I. "My Intellectual Path." *New York Review of Books,* 1998, *45*(8), 53–60.

Bickman, L. "A Continuum of Care: More Is Not Always Better." *American Psychologist,* 1996, *57*(7), pp. 689–701.

Bryk, A. S. (ed.). *Stakeholder-Based Evaluation.* New Directions for Program Evaluation, no. 17. San Francisco: Jossey-Bass, 1983.

Campbell, D. T. "Experiments as Arguments." *Evaluation Studies Review Annual,* 1982, *7,* 117–127.

Caplan, N. "A Minimal Set of Conditions Necessary for the Utilization of Social Science Knowledge in Policy Formulation at the National Level." In C. H. Weiss (ed.), *Using Social Research in Public Policy Making.* Lexington Mass.: Heath, 1977.

Caplan, N., Morrison, A., and Stambaugh, R. J. *The Use of Social Science Knowledge in Policy Decisions at the National Level: A Report to Respondents.* Ann Arbor, Mich.: Institute for Social Research, University of Michigan, 1975.

Cohen, B. *The Press and Foreign Policy.* Princeton, N.J.: Princeton University Press, 1963.

Cohen, M. D., March, J. G., and Olsen, J. P. "A Garbage Can Model of Organizational Choice." *Administrative Science Quarterly,* 1982, Volume 17, pp. 1–25.

Fishkin, J. S. *The Voice of the People: Public Opinion and Democracy.* New Haven, Conn.: Yale University Press, 1995.

Funnell, S. "Developing and Using a Program Theory Matrix for Program Evaluation and Performance Monitoring." In A. Petrosino, P. J. Rogers, T. A. Huebner, and T. A. Hacsi (eds.), *Program Theory Evaluation: Surveying the Field of Practice.* New Directions for Evaluation, no. 87. San Francisco: Jossey-Bass, 2000.

Galston, W. A. "Value Pluralism and Liberal Political Theory." *American Political Science Review,* 1999, *93*(4), 769–778.

Glazer, N. "How Social Problems Are Born." *Public Interest,* 1994, *115,* 31–44.

Gueron, J. M. "Learning About Welfare Reform: Lessons from State-Based Evaluations." In D. J. Rog and D. Fournier (eds.), *Progress and Future Directions in Evaluation: Perspectives on Theory, Practice, and Methods.* New Directions for Evaluation, no. 76. San Francisco: Jossey-Bass, 1997.

Habermas, J. "Three Normative Models of Democracy." In Seyla Benhabib (ed.), *Democracy and Difference: Contesting the Boundaries of the Political.* Princeton, N.J.: Princeton University Press, 1996.

Henry, G. T., and Julnes, G. "Values and Realist Evaluation." In G. T. Henry, G. Julnes, and M. M. Mark (eds.), *Realist Evaluation: An Emerging Theory in Support of Practice.* New Directions for Evaluation, no. 78. San Francisco: Jossey-Bass, 1998.

Hilgartner, S., and Bosk, C. "The Rise and Fall of Social Problems: A Public Arena's Model." *American Journal of Sociology,* 1988, *94*(1), 53–78.

Hurley, S. *Natural Reasons: Personality and Polity.* New York: Oxford University Press, 1989.

Ivengar, S., Peters, M. D., and Kinder, D. R. "Experimental Demonstrations of the 'Not-So-Minimal' Consequences of Television News Programs." *American Political Science Review,* 1982, *76,* 848–857.

Jones, B. D., True, J. L., and Baumgartner, F. R. "Does Incrementalism Stem from Consensus or from Institutional Gridlock?" *American Journal of Political Science,* 1997, *41,* 1319–1339.

Kendler, H. H. "The Role of Value in the World of Psychology." *American Psychologist,* 1999, 54(10), pp. 828–835.

Kingdon, J. *Agendas, Alternatives, and Public Policies.* (2nd ed.) New York: HarperCollins, 1995.

Knorr, K. D. "Policymakers' Use of Social Science Knowledge: Symbolic or Instrumental?" In C. H. Weiss (ed.), *Using Social Research in Public Policy Making.* Lexington, Mass.: Heath, 1977.

Kosicki, G. M. "Problems and Opportunities in Agenda-Setting Research." *Journal of Communications,* 1993, *43*(2), 100–127.

Krosnick, J. A., and Brannon, L. A. "The Impact of the Gulf War on the Ingredients of Presidential Evaluations: Multidimensional Effects of Political Involvement." *American Political Science Review,* 1993, *87*(4), 963–975.

Krosnick, J. A., and Kinder, D. R. "Altering the Foundations of Support for the President Through Priming." *American Political Science Review,* 1989, *84*(2), 497–512.

Lindbloom, C. E. *The Policy-Making Process.* Englewood Cliffs, N.J.: Prentice Hall, 1968.

Majone, G. *Evidence, Argument, and Persuasion in the Policy Process.* New Haven, Conn.: Yale University Press, 1989.

Mark, M. M., Henry, G. T., and Julnes, G. *Evaluation: An Integrated Framework for Understanding, Guiding, and Improving Policies and Programs.* San Francisco: Jossey-Bass, 2000.

McCombs, M. E., and Shaw, D. "The Agenda-Setting Function of Mass Media." *Public Opinion Quarterly,* 1972, *36,* 176–185.

Monroe, A. "Public Opinion and Public Policy, 1980–1993." *Public Opinion Quarterly,* 1998, 62(1), 6–27.

Nachmias, D., and Henry, G. T. "The Utilization of Evaluation Research: Problems and Prospects." In D. Nachmias (ed.), *The Practice of Policy Evaluation.* New York: St. Martin's Press, 1979.

Nelson, B. J. *Making an Issue of Child Abuse.* Chicago: University of Chicago Press, 1984.

Page, B. I. *Who Deliberates? Mass Media in Modern Democracy.* Chicago: University of Chicago Press, 1996.

Page, B. I., and Shapiro, R. Y. *The Rational Public: Fifty Years of Trends in Americans' Policy Preferences.* Chicago: University of Chicago Press, 1992.

Patton, M. Q. *Utilization-Focused Evaluation.* Thousand Oaks, Calif.: Sage, 1978.

Patton, M. Q. *Utilization-Focused Evaluation: The New Century Text.* (3rd ed.) Thousand Oaks, Calif.: Sage, 1997.

Patton, M. Q., and others. "In Search of Impact: An Analysis of the Utilization of Federal Health Evaluation Research." In C. H. Weiss (ed.), *Using Social Research in Public Policy Making.* Lexington, Mass.: Heath, 1977.

Rog, D. J. "A Methodological Analysis of Evaluability Assessment." Unpublished doctoral dissertation, Vanderbilt University, Nashville, Tenn., 1985.

Rutman, L. *Planning Useful Evaluations: Evaluability Assessment.* Thousand Oaks, Calif.: Sage, 1988.

Scarr, S. "American Child Care Today." *American Psychologist,* 1998, volume 53, pp. 95–108.

Scheirer, M. A. (ed.). "A User's Guide to Program Templates: A New Tool for Evaluation Program Content." New Directions for Evaluation, no. 72. San Francisco: Jossey-Bass, 1996.

Shulha, L. M., and Cousins, J. B. "Evaluation Use: Theory, Research, and Practice Since 1986." *Evaluation Practice,* 1997, *18*(3), 195–208.

Shulock, N. "The Paradox of Policy Analysis: If It Is Not Used, Why Do We Produce So Much of It?" *Journal of Policy Analysis and Management,* 1999, *18*(2), 226–244.

Stimson, J. A. *Public Opinion in America: Moods, Cycles, and Swings.* (2nd ed.) Boulder, Colo.: Westview Press, 1998.

Stufflebeam, D. L. "Foundational Models for Twenty-First Century Program Evaluation." New Directions for Evaluation, no. 89. San Francisco: Jossey-Bass, forthcoming.

Weikhart, D. P., and Schweinhart, L. J. "The High/Scope Preschool Curriculum Comparison Study Through Age 23." *Early Childhood Research Quarterly,* 1997, *12*(2), 117–143.

Weiss, C. H. "The Stakeholder Approach to Evaluation: Origins and Promise." In A. S. Bryk (ed.), *Stakeholder-Based Evaluation.* New Directions for Program Evaluation, no. 17. San Francisco: Jossey-Bass, 1983.

Weiss, C. H., and Bucuvalas, M. J. "The Challenge of Social Research to Decision Making." In C. H. Weiss (ed.), *Using Social Research in Public Policy Making.* Lexington Mass.: Heath, 1977.

Wholey, J. "Assessing the Feasibility and Likely Usefulness of Evaluation." In J. S. Wholey, H. P. Hatry, and K. E. Newcomer (eds.), *Handbook of Practical Program Evaluation.* San Francisco: Jossey-Bass, 1994.

Zhu, J. H. "Issue Competition and Attention Distraction: A Zero-Sum Theory of Agenda-Setting." *Journalism Quarterly,* 1992, *69*(4), 825–836.

GARY T. HENRY is a professor in the Andrew Young School of Policy Studies and Departments of Political Science and Educational Policy Studies, Georgia State University, where he also directs the Applied Research Center.

7

This chapter recaps some of the central insights of the preceding chapters as they relate to historical marker events from the past three decades that have influenced the evaluation profession and expanded our notions of use.

Evaluation Use at the Threshold of the Twenty-First Century

Valerie J. Caracelli

The intellectual roots of social program evaluation, the prominent arena of the evaluation discipline, are usually traced to the 1960s, the era of the Great Society, and to what the evaluation discipline has referred to as Donald Campbell's Experimenting Society. In 1971, Alice Rivlin, a notable economist with extensive government service and a senior fellow at the Brookings Institution during that time, evaluated the evaluators, essentially giving a report card on the progress of analysts in improving the basis for public decisions on social action programs. Questions about the utility of the profession were raised: What contribution had evaluation made? Were insights gained about what needs social programs had fulfilled? With what kinds of decisions had evaluation proved helpful? Rivlin found the following: there had been considerable progress in identifying social problems and in estimating who would gain if social programs were successful, and there had been little progress in comparing the benefits of different social programs (for example, "the analysts cannot say whether another million dollars would be better spent to cure cancer or to teach poor children to read" [p. vii]). More recently, Daniel Patrick Moynihan (1996) considered thirty years of social policy and concluded that we still have "miles to go" (p. 220). Indirectly, the literature on evaluation utilization, or currently evaluation use, speaks to perceptions about the viability of the evaluation profession in these and other policy contexts.

Note: The opinions expressed in this chapter represent those of the author and should not be construed as the policy or position of the U.S. General Accounting Office.

At the threshold of the twenty-first century, the problems facing society remain extraordinarily complex and difficult. Beauregard (1998), in tracing past and present social policy research, finds that Campbell's critics have argued that his approach had only a rudimentary sense of context, which was insufficient for how society might undertake and adopt widespread reform. Such critics (for example, Dunn, 1990; Knorr-Cetina, 1981; Majone, 1989; and Wildavsky, 1979) have argued that "all social action and understanding is socially negotiated and context dependent and that reform is as much a matter of argumentation and practical reasoning as it is of experimentation and deductive representation" (p. 212). From Beauregard's point of view, these critics fail to specify the dynamics of a deeper context, one that considers ethnic makeup, economic conditions, political balance of power, age of the population, quality of the environment, and other relevant contextual factors. "What has not been given sufficient attention . . . is the intersection of social diversity and space and the increased salience of cultural differences in political settings" (p. 220). Evaluation today takes place in this kind of complex social context. In addition, evaluation practitioners embrace different paradigms, perspectives, and values; they conduct evaluation for different purposes, take on different roles, and favor a diverse array of practices. It is today's complex and differentiated context that the authors of this volume on evaluation use address.

This chapter engages this context by connecting the discussions in this volume to selected *marker events* in evaluation's recent history, events that have influenced our profession and expanded our notions of use.[1] Presented within broader themes, these markers are used to organize the discussion and represent processes that began before and continue after the time frame indicated. They also represent shifts in the course and direction of the profession that continue to influence our current conceptions of evaluation practice.[2]

Theme One: Multiplicity in Evaluation

Over the past thirty years, the evaluation profession has experienced an increasing differentiation of evaluation theory and practice. The accommodation of different philosophies, perspectives, values, and practices also accompanied and continues to require a more differentiated understanding of evaluation use.

Fundamentals of Critical Multiplism (1985 . . .). From its inception, the discipline of evaluation has been concerned with the quality of research and has placed emphasis on securing valid and trustworthy information. Campbell and Fiske's conceptualization of *multiple operationalism* and its effects on strengthening inferences from studies through procedures for assessing convergent and discriminant validity, which was put forth in their classic article (1959), remains an important aspect of today's evaluation practice (Crano, 2000). Cook (1985), using the roots of the *multitrait-*

multimethod matrix, elaborated a more general strategy of multiple triangulation among theories, perspectives, political and value frameworks, measures, methods, and multiple analytical strategies. The explication of method bias and the ensuing strategies used to offset potential bias were intended to strengthen the plausibility of knowledge claims. Cook's *critical multiplism* was founded on the basic premise of the uncertainty of scientific knowledge and the belief that a general strategy of diversity in all aspects of inquiry could enhance validity. Dunn (1994) adapts Cook's framework for policy inquiry and links it to generating more useful knowledge in the social and policy sciences. Critical multiplism is viewed as increasing the likelihood that evaluation findings for policy assessment, in a political arena where competing interests advance their own agendas, will be used correctly. However, use may still occur in situations in which program goals, timely need for information, and resource constraints result in less rigor and attention to validity (Shadish, Cook, and Leviton, 1991). The importance of the credibility of information persists in conversations about how politics factors into the policies and programs that evaluation is expected to influence (Chelimsky, 1998; Datta, 2000).

The Paradigm Wars (1980–1995). An aspect of multiplicity that is characteristic of the field of evaluation is the evaluator's paradigmatic perspective—that is, his or her basic beliefs, assumptions, and values about the aim of social inquiry and the nature of social knowing (Schwandt, 1997). For about fifteen years, the paradigm debate focused mainly on distinctions between what were described early on as the qualitative and the quantitative paradigms (Reichardt and Cook, 1979).[3] Patton (1997) describes Stake's *responsive evaluation* (1975) as an alternative to the dominant experimental paradigm and one that influenced evaluators to think about the connection between methods and use. The *paradigm wars* reflected profound differences in diverse philosophical and ideological positions held by the evaluation community (Guba, 1990; Lincoln and Guba, 1985). The dialogues that ensued around alternative paradigms broadened the influence of evaluation to encompass a wide variety of perspectives and practices (Greene, 1994, 2000). Cook (1997) observes that ultimately these dialogues contributed to legitimating qualitative methods and other forms of inquiry. Qualitative approaches furnished useful knowledge about program theory and helped evaluators understand program context, describe implementation, illuminate processes that may have brought about program effects, and identify unintended consequences. He also notes that they are relevant to reducing uncertainty about causal propositions and for generalizing to specific populations.

The paradigm debates also resulted in more attention to studies using multiple and mixed methods, showing the intertwining of this marker event with triangulation and the multiplist framework that grew out of the multitrait-multimethod matrix (Greene, Caracelli, and Graham, 1989; Greene and Caracelli, 1997). Benefits from mixed-method studies can include enhanced validity and credibility of inferences, greater comprehensiveness of findings, more insightful understandings, and increased value consciousness and diversity (Greene, Benjamin, Goodyear, and Lowe, 1999). Today, overall, these benefits broaden the influence of evaluation and are sought after in the spectrum of diverse evaluation practices.

Multiplicity and Evaluation Use. The theme of multiplicity is a broad and encompassing one in evaluation. As depicted in these marker events, it includes much more than the evaluator's methodological tool chest. It encompasses different worldviews, values, perspectives, and opinions on the purposes evaluation serves. Multiplicity is reflected in this volume's writing on use in several ways. First, the construct of use itself has multiple attributes. Kirkhart's integrated theory of influence represents an incorporation of past understandings of use based on evaluation literature, as well as providing a deeper, more developed and differentiated construct of use in light of the changing circumstances of the field and its increasing diversity. The shift in terminology from *use* to *influence* creates a broader framework that allows for multiple perspectives. Evaluation influence is conceptualized along three dimensions—source, addressing results-based and process-based influence; intention, addressing intended and unintended influence; and time, addressing influence that occurs during evaluation, at the end of evaluation, and in the future. Taken together, they represent influence as nonlinear, multifaceted, multidirectional, and interactive.

Second, although sharing a common focus on use, the authors in this volume have multiple and diverse views on the purpose served by evaluation, views that in turn relate to differences in their constructions of use. For example, Henry views the purpose of evaluation as social betterment. With this purpose, credibility is key, if use as a future consequence of the evaluation is to serve as a mechanism for achieving social betterment. Henry cautions that beginning an evaluation with the goal of use may result in the evaluation's losing the credibility necessary to persuade. For Preskill and Torres, a different perspective is given when evaluation is considered in organizational contexts in which evaluative inquiry serves as a mechanism for transformative learning. Use is thus built into the process of the evaluation. Given this purpose, the authors' perspectives on methodological rigor are conditioned by other factors—for example, a compromise to rigor may be worth considering for situations in which information may not be available or when information that can be made available will be sufficient to be used as a basis for dialogue, reflection, and learning. With nuanced differences, the chapters by Shulha and by Rossman and Rallis also cast evaluation as learning. A theory of evaluation influence and use must be broad enough to encompass these different perspectives, and others, and be capable of filling diverse niches of evaluation practice.

Third, the authors in this volume bring to the study of evaluation use concepts from a number of other disciplines. Multiplicity is inherent in the knowledge base of the field. Evaluation as a transdiscipline (Scriven, 1991) informs the practice of other disciplines, and evaluation's own theory and substantive knowledge base has been informed by the multidisciplinary makeup of the profession. For example, although Kirkhart closely adheres to the evaluation literature, her background in community psychology and social work is reflected in the broad integrative perspective that is brought to bear on her depiction of a theory of influence that bridges different paradigms and levels of context. Knowledge about organizational development is incorporated in four of the chapters, those by Preskill and Torres; Brett, Hill-Mead, and Wu; Rossman and Rallis; and Shulha. Preskill and Torres ground their discussion in the adult learning literature and also incorporate concepts from organizational learning and organizational change. Brett, Hill-Mead, and Wu add a focus drawn from the literature on late adolescence in the study of human development. Shulha draws from education and student assessment, as well as on action research. Cognitive development and constructivist learning theory are integral aspects of the chapter developed by Rossman and Rallis, including theories from action science pertinent to appreciative inquiry. Political science and communications inform Henry's discussion on agenda setting; his discussion about values is informed by philosophy, psychology, and political science. This cross-fertilization among disciplines of the social sciences and evaluation has characterized the evolution of the evaluation profession and its natural affinity with multiplicity.

Theme Two: Expansion of the Evaluator's Role in a Broad Array of Contexts

The marker events in this theme relate to a more diverse set of roles that have become part of the evaluator's repertoire over time. Weiss (1998) traces the expansion of the evaluator role from dispassionate outsider to coinvestigator with program staff, who assumes a variety of roles that require degrees of engagement with stakeholders. She cites several reasons for the change, including problems with results-based use that resulted from mistrust of the evaluator in the past, a recognition that the major use of evaluation results was for purposes of program improvement, and the knowledge that the evaluation itself could be an intervention and instrument of social change. Weiss links the ideas behind stakeholder involvement and empowerment approaches to action research in the 1940s. Evaluator roles today are described by such terms as *facilitator, problem solver, educator, coach,* and *critical friend.*

These roles evolve out of changing circumstances and a broadened array of contexts in which evaluation inquiry is conducted. In social policy domains, the emphasis on federal control over programs that characterized evaluation in the 1960s has shifted to more flexible programming offered at the state and local levels. For example, Title 1 of the Elementary and Secondary Education Act is essentially a funding mechanism. It authorizes aid to local educational agencies (LEAs) for the education of disadvantaged children, with latitude in allowing LEAs to select curriculum and staff, instructional approach, and other aspects of the program (Riddle, 2000). Similar shifts from federal to state program control have occurred in other federal programs, notably Temporary Assistance to Needy Families, which replaced the entitlement program of Aid to Families with Dependent Children with a fixed block grant for state-designed programs (Burke, 2000). The complexity of social problems results in multifaceted interventions designed to produce multiple outcomes at various micro and macro levels of context. In addition, today evaluators work not only in the public policy arena but also in the private and philanthropic sectors and in various organizational contexts, from large corporate training programs to local, non-profit community initiatives. Evaluators' roles have evolved in response to conducting inquiry in an increasing variety of milieus. A more sophisticated understanding of these diverse contexts is necessary to maximize both process and results-based use.

Stakeholder-Based, Collaborative, and Participatory Evaluation Approaches (Mid-1970s . . .). The origins of stakeholder-based evaluation, the inclusion in the evaluation of those who make decisions about the program or whose lives are affected by the program and its evaluation, is discussed by Weiss (1983) in a *New Directions for Program Evaluation* volume devoted to what was then an innovative approach to evaluation, which was introduced in the late 1970s. The justification for stakeholder involvement was related to the idea that it could increase the use of evaluation results in decision making. Patton (1997) highlights much of the subsequent and substantiating literature under the importance to utilization of the personal factor. However, the approach represented a shift in the consciousness of the profession. As Weiss noted at the time, "Realization of the legitimacy of competing interests and the multiplicity of perspectives and willingness to place evaluation at the service of diverse groups are important intellectual advances" (p. 11).

Cousins and Whitmore (1998) note that forms and applications of collaborative research and inquiry became ascendant in the evaluation field in the mid-1970s, yet their history can be traced to large-scale community action movements in the 1960s and even to earlier movements, including those undertaken in developing countries. Their framework compares collaborative and participatory evaluation approaches on a set of dimensions related to control, level, and range of participation. The framework also allows for differentiating forms of collaborative inquiry across two broad-based categorizations reflecting *practical* or *transformative participatory evaluation*. Practical participatory evaluation is focused on evaluation use, whereas transformative participatory evaluation is focused on the empowerment of oppressed groups.

Brisolara (1998) outlines the central tenets of participatory evaluation and emphasizes that the "process of the evaluation (and what is learned throughout the process) is an important outcome" (p. 25). Also characteristic of this genre of evaluation practices is the importance of including stakeholders, sustaining dialogue among diverse voices to gain a holistic understanding of the program, and the various roles assumed by the evaluator, such as facilitator, change agent, and educator. Taken collectively, such approaches by virtue of their inclusive stance are considered "utilization friendly" (p. 35). But the type of use promoted across the broad-based categorizations of practical or transformative participatory evaluation is different, from user-focused to openly ideological use, respectively.

Theory-Based Evaluations (1980s . . .). Theory-based evaluations reflect the movement away from "black box" evaluations. They represent a shift toward greater understanding of the substantive theory of the problem, an emphasis on the conceptual relationship between program implementation and expected outcomes, and expanded roles for the evaluator beyond detached observer. Weiss (1998) elaborates on how theories of change can serve as a guide to evaluation; she cites advantages to program designers, practitioners, program managers, and funders and to policymakers and the public. Theory-based evaluation provides explanations in the form of stories that can be more convincing than statistical findings alone and "may stand a better chance of influencing the course of future policy" (p. 68). Logic models, a visual way of depicting program theory, are commonly used in evaluability assessments (Wholey, 1994) and other outcome studies (Cooksy, Gill, and Kelly, forthcoming).

Patton's (1997) user-focused theory of action approach involves developing program theory with program stakeholders. Helping program staff or decision makers reframe vague notions into an articulated theory of action enhances communication and serves an educational purpose. In this evaluation scenario, it is the evaluation process that is used to improve a program (p. 229). Theory-based evaluations therefore take into account evaluation process use and the more traditional emphasis on results-based use. Today, even in field experiment modes of evaluation, planned variation approaches—a type of theory-based evaluation—are advocated as a form of collaborative evaluation research that is useful to program operators and can build a knowledge base to develop better programs (Yeh, 2000).

Evaluator's Role and Use. Perhaps imperceptible-at-the-time but nonetheless dramatic changes in the practice of evaluation are reflected in these marker events. These changes in practice expanded the roles and responsibilities of evaluators, with concomitant changes occurring in our understanding of the multidimensional aspects of use. Kirkhart's integrated theory of influence clearly accounts for these influences and is intended to provide a reconceptualization that shifts a prior focus on results-based use to a model that can account for a parallel treatment of process use. Process forms of use are especially apparent in several of the chapters in this volume, and the implications for the roles of the evaluator are many.

Again, expanded evaluator roles are intertwined with broadened evaluation contexts, such as organizational (Preskill and Torres) and school-university (Rossman and Rallis; Shulha). The macro societal perspective that is addressed in the chapter by Henry takes into consideration the changing social policy context. In Brett, Hill-Mead, and Wu's discussion of City Year, a bridge from macro to local site contexts allows for an examination of both process and results-based use that cuts across different system levels in a cultural context committed to change and transformative learning. The case study also illustrates the utility of Kirkhart's integrated theory of influence along the dimensions of intention, source of influence, and time.

The chapters in this volume offer a wide array of evaluator roles across these diverse contexts. Preskill and Torres discuss evaluative inquiry in organizational contexts that result in evaluation use as transformative learning. This outcome results from a process that is collaborative, dialogic, and action oriented. To facilitate transformative learning in organizations, the evaluator may engage in a variety of roles—for example, educator, consultant, interpreter, mediator, emancipator. Shulha's discussion of evaluative inquiry as a foundation for school-university partnerships is analyzed in light of Kirkhart's integrated theory of influence. The participatory partnership between academics and teachers results in an inquiry process that supports ongoing individual and collective learning. Shulha reports that the process resulted in teachers' reconceptualizing their role in shaping the organization and communicating the depth of their understanding to others. The evaluator served as mentor and as learning partner in the joint inquiry process that resulted in these outcomes. The chapter by Rossman and Rallis views stakeholders as partners in the construction of knowledge. The evaluator and the primary partner, the program leadership, engage in a process of learning through dialogue, exploration, and critique in which use is action. In this partnership, the evaluator serves such roles as teacher, resource, and facilitator and may be looked on as "old friend." In critical inquiry, use is inherent in the inquiry process itself, and the outcome of learning has the potential to result in social change.

Rossman and Rallis also note that the critical inquiry process probes deep assumptions about program theory and about the relationship between program activities and outcomes. Brett, Hill-Mead, and Wu found that in a consultant role, the new evaluation department, Research and Systematic Learning, engaged City Year staff in the process of developing logic models that resulted in assisting staff in designing their services. Henry also finds that logic models, among other types of assessments, are useful in providing feedback on adapting a particular course of action that can lead to the common good, one of the necessary functions in pursuing social betterment as the goal of evaluation.

Theme Three: Emerging Marker Events at the Threshold of the New Century

Changes in technology and in the global evaluation community relate to challenges that face the evaluation profession in the twenty-first century.

These challenges have implications for the practice of evaluation and the use and potential misuse of evaluation information.

Information Technology Changes—Data Storage Capacity, Record Linkage, Multimedia (1990s . . .). Notwithstanding the contribution of social scientific and statistical research in affecting social policy in years prior to the 1960s, increasing computer data processing capacity paved the way for the wider use of surveys, based on scientific sampling of the U.S. populations, to understand the scope of social problems and to inform policies that address the allocation of resources (Rivlin, 1971). Today there is an exponential growth of electronic records (gathered and maintained by federal, state, and local governments and by private sector organizations). Increased data storage and computer capacity allow for the analysis of these records. A by-product is the potential for record linkage; for example, data on a set of individuals or organizations may be combined with another set of records that describe the same entities. Record linkage means that existing evaluative information can be built on and expanded; for example, data on individuals participating in an intervention program may be matched to outcome data kept in state employment records or local law enforcement records. Although there are benefits to these developments, there are also challenges associated with protecting the privacy and confidentiality of data on program participants (Garfinkel, 2000; U.S. General Accounting Office, forthcoming). In order to increase access to date, one trend in the latter part of the twentieth century was to make available public use data sets that had been stripped of respondents' personal identifiers. However, additional data suppressions may be necessary for public use data sets because certain variables (such as race, occupation, and state of residence) in combination could allow for the identification of individuals. Publicly available data may suppress data on subgroups for whom evaluation information is already inadequate, potentially biasing subsequent analyses. These issues have important implications for maximizing evaluators' access to information to conduct research and for the subsequent use and potential for misuse of data.

Another challenge in evaluation research related to conducting inquiry and disseminating findings stems from the use of multimedia as an adjunct to traditional modes of gathering and communicating information. Today the Internet allows for conducting e-mail questionnaires, Web-based surveys, and focus groups (Dillman, 1999; Watt, 1999). Other computer-mediated approaches allow text data, observations, photographs, graphic design, video, and audio to be integrated to produce evaluation reports that can reach a worldwide audience within days of report completion. As discussed in Gay and Bennington (1999), these potent new information technologies and computer-mediated communication tools are transforming organizational settings. Design strategies for the presentation of information raise questions about how the integrity of data can be maintained "in the face of complex and animated representations of data" (Tufte, 1997, p. 9). These new challenges raise new concerns about the power of data display that figure prominently in issues of the use and misuse of evaluation information.

Global Evaluation Community. Today many problems of great concern to the evaluation community are global in nature—for example, global migration patterns, environmental issues, disease epidemics, the population explosion, and financial institutions and markets. The American Evaluation Association is now one of a number of national organizations that represent evaluation activities. Although international evaluation is not new, the initiative for developing a framework for cooperation among the different national evaluation societies has only recently been undertaken.[4] Bamberger (2000) calls for a closer exchange between U.S. evaluators and their colleagues from developing countries. Evaluations of development programs are being conducted in almost every country in the developing world. Bamberger cites some promising approaches in evaluation design and utilization (for example, participatory evaluation, integration of quantitative and qualitative methods, use of longitudinal socioeconomic data sets). In many of these cases, cooperation with the United States could be mutually beneficial. Smith and Jang (2000) note that our understanding of cultural differences continues to improve as U.S. evaluators work in international and domestic cross-cultural settings. Using an example of evaluation work conducted in Korea, they caution that our traditional notions of establishing validity and our criteria for judging an evaluation's utility are likely to differ from those of other cultures. The technology that allows evaluators to share and use information across the world needs to be accompanied by a sensitivity to cultural differences and an understanding of different environmental and contextual factors.

Use in the Twenty-First Century. During the last thirty years, there have been shifts in thinking that have influenced the practice of evaluation and expanded our understanding of the construct of use. Yet, to date, there had been no integration of these changing conceptions of use. Kirkhart's integrated theory of influence responds to this need. The other chapter authors elaborate on various aspects of this theory, in particular on issues pertaining to evaluative inquiry and process use. The ideas presented in this volume are yoked in this concluding chapter to selected historical markers that pertain to multiplicity and expanding evaluator roles in a broad array of contexts.

At the threshold of the twenty-first century, the use of evaluation will also be greatly influenced by changes in information technology. Preskill and Torres find visual displays useful for group processing of data, which can serve as opportunities for transformative learning when questions and assumptions are clarified and findings are collectively interpreted. However, with these new technologies caution is required. Henry speaks to the issue of information disclosure and the potential under certain situations, particularly when persuasion becomes the inquiry purpose, to compromise evidence. In Kirkhart's framework, examining source, intention, and time allows for engaging in dialogue that can illuminate both the beneficial and the detrimental consequences that are potentially present in how these new information technologies are used.

The twenty-first century also brings trends such as globalization and new initiatives that can foster greater cooperation among countries in a new global evaluation community. As Shulha recounts in the cross-cultural school-university partnership study, shared experiences do not necessarily result in shared meanings. Here again, our conceptions about evaluation influence and use are likely to be challenged. Kirkhart's theory of influence provides a framework that allows for the incorporation of different paradigms and the opportunity to advance dialogue by encouraging the inspection of language and meaning. The ideas about evaluation influence or use advanced in this volume ideally can serve as an impetus for further inquiry that continues to advance our understanding of this fundamental construct in evaluation theory and practice.

Notes

1. The notion of marker or life events is also used in life-span development. A critical life events framework provides a conceptual focus for developing preventive strategies and more effective and efficient interventions (See Danish, Smyer, and Nowack, 1980).

2. Evaluation practice in the form of specific studies can also serve as marker events. Several of these studies (for example, "The Coleman Report" and "The Consortium of Longitudinal Studies") were outlined in an earlier presentation at the 1998 annual conference of the American Evaluation Association. Other marker events related to advances in analytical techniques also have implications for evaluation use—for example, research synthesis and meta-analysis and multilevel modeling techniques.

3. Cook (1997) frames a fifteen-year period for the paradigm wars in evaluation. However, the debates were already under way and were brought to evaluation when sociologists entered the field in the 1970s.

4. In February 2000, the W. K. Kellogg Foundation sponsored a meeting in Barbados, and representatives from fifteen national and multinational organizations convened to discuss evaluation issues that cut across national boundaries.

References

Bamberger, M. "The Evaluation of International Development Programs: A View from the Front." *American Journal of Evaluation,* 2000, *21*(1), 95–102.

Beauregard, R. A. "The Deeper Context of the Experimenting Society." In W. N. Dunn (ed.), *The Experimenting Society: Essays in Honor of Donald T. Campbell.* Policy Studies Review Annual, vol. 11. New Brunswick, N.J.: Transaction, 1998.

Brisolara, S. "The History of Participatory Evaluation and Current Debates in the Field." In E. Whitmore (ed.), *Understanding and Practicing Participatory Evaluation.* New Directions for Evaluation, no. 80. San Francisco: Jossey-Bass, 1998.

Burke, V. "Welfare Reform: An Issue Overview." Washington, D.C.: U.S. Congressional Research Service, Aug. 11, 2000.

Campbell, D. T., and Fiske, D. W. "Convergent and Discriminant Validation by the Multitrait-Multimethod Matrix." *Psychological Bulletin,* 1959, *56,* 81–105.

Chelimsky, E. "The Role of Experience in Formulating Theories of Evaluation Practice." *American Journal of Evaluation,* 1998, *19*(1), 35–55.

Cook, T. D. "Postpositivist Critical Multiplism." In R. L. Sholtland and M. M. Mark (eds.), *Social Science and Social Policy.* Thousand Oaks, Calif.: Sage, 1985.

Cook, T. D. "Lessons Learned in Evaluation Over the Past Twenty-Five Years." In E. Chelimsky and W. R. Shadish, Jr. (eds.), *Evaluation for the 21st Century: A Handbook.* Thousand Oaks, Calif.: Sage, 1997.

Cooksy, L. J., Gill, P., Kelly, P. A. "The Program Logic Model as an Integrative Evaluation and Program Planning Framework for a Multimethod Evaluation." *In Evaluation and Program Planning.* Forthcoming.

Cousins, J. B., and Whitmore, E. "Framing Participatory Evaluation." In E. Whitmore (ed.), *Understanding and Practicing Participatory Evaluation.* New Directions for Evaluation, no. 80. San Francisco: Jossey-Bass, 1998.

Crano, W. D. "The Multitrait-Multimethod Matrix as Synopsis and Recapitulation of Campbell's Views on the Proper Conduct of Social Inquiry." In L. Bickman (ed.), *Research Design: Donals Campbell's Legacy.* Vol. 2. Thousand Oaks, Calif.: Sage, 2000.

Danish, S. J., Smyer, M. A., and Nowack, C. A. "Developmental Intervention: Enhancing Life-Event Processes." In P. B. Baltes and O. G. Brim, Jr. (eds.), *Life-Span Development and Behavior,* 1980, *3,* pp. 339–366.

Datta, L-e. "Seriously Seeking Fairness: Strategies for Crafting Non-Partisan Evaluations in a Partisan World." *American Journal of Evaluation,* 2000, *21*(1), 1–14.

Dillman, D. *Mail and Internet Surveys: The Tailored Design Method.* (2nd ed.) New York: Wiley, 1999.

Dunn, W. N. "Justifying Policy Arguments." *Evaluation and Program Planning,* 1990, *13,* 321–329.

Dunn, W. N. *Public Policy Analysis: An Introduction.* (2nd ed.) Englewood Cliffs, N.J.: Prentice Hall, 1994.

Garfinkel, S. *Database Nation: The Death of Privacy in the 21st Century.* Sebastopol, Calif.: O'Reilly & Associates, 2000.

Gay, G., and Bennington, T. L. (eds.). *Information Technologies in Evaluation: Social, Moral, Epistemological, and Practical Implications.* New Directions for Evaluation, no. 84. San Francisco: Jossey-Bass, 1999.

Greene, J. C. "Qualitative Program Evaluation: Practice and Promise." In N. K. Denzin and Y. S. Lincoln (eds.), *Handbook of Qualitative Research.* Thousand Oaks, Calif.: Sage, 1994.

Greene, J. C. "Understanding Social Programs Through Evaluation." In N. K Denzin and Y. S. Lincoln (eds.), *Handbook of Qualitative Research.* (2nd ed.) Thousand Oaks, Calif.: Sage, 2000.

Greene, J. C., Benjamin, L., Goodyear, L., and Lowe, S. "The Merits of Mixing Methods in Applied Social Research." Paper presented at the Association for Public Policy Analysis and Management conference, Washington, D.C., Nov. 1999.

Greene, J. C., and Caracelli, V. J. "Defining and Describing the Paradigm Issue in Mixed-Method Evaluation." In J. C. Greene and V. J. Caracelli (eds.), *Advances in Mixed-Method Evaluation: The Challenges and Benefits of Integrating Diverse Paradigms.* New Directions for Evaluation, no. 74. San Francisco: Jossey-Bass, 1997.

Greene, J. C., Caracelli, V. J., and Graham, W. F. "Toward a Conceptual Framework for Mixed-Method Evaluation Designs. *Educational Evaluation and Policy Analysis,* 1989, *11*(3), 255–274.

Guba, E. G. (ed.). *The Paradigm Dialog.* Thousand Oaks, Calif.: Sage, 1990.

Knorr-Cetina, K. D. "Time and Context in Practical Action." *Knowledge: Creation, Diffusion, Utilization,* 1981, *3*(2), 143–165.

Lincoln, Y. S., and Guba, E. G. *Naturalistic Inquiry.* Thousand Oaks, Calif.: Sage, 1985.

Majone, G. *Evidence, Argument, and Persuasion in the Policy Process.* New Haven, Conn.: Yale University Press, 1989.

Moynihan, D. P. *Miles to Go: A Personal History of Social Policy.* Cambridge, Mass.: Harvard University Press, 1996.

Patton, M. Q. *Utilization-Focused Evaluation: The New Century Text.* (3rd ed.) Thousand Oaks, Calif.: Sage, 1997.

Reichardt, C. S., and Cook, T. D. "Beyond Qualitative Versus Quantitative Methods." In T. D. Cook and C. S. Reichardt (eds.), *Qualitative and Quantitative Methods in Evaluation Research.* Thousand Oaks, Calif.: Sage, 1979.

Riddle, W. "Education for the Disadvantaged: Elementary and Secondary Education Act Title I Reauthorization Issues." Washington, D.C.: U.S. Government Printing Office, July 31, 2000.

Rivlin, A. M. *Systematic Thinking for Social Action.* Washington, D.C.: Brookings Institution. 1971.

Schwandt, T. A. *Qualitative Inquiry: A Dictionary of Terms.* Thousand Oaks, Calif.: Sage, 1997.

Scriven, M. *Evaluation Thesaurus.* (4th ed.) Thousand Oaks, Calif.: Sage, 1991.

Shadish, W. R., Jr., Cook, T. D., and Leviton, L. C. *Foundations of Program Evaluation: Theories of Practice.* Thousand Oaks, Calif.: Sage, 1991.

Smith, N. L., and Jang, S. "Cultural Influences on Utility and Validity in Evaluation Practice." Paper presented at the American Psychological Association, Washington, D.C., August 2000.

Stake, R. E. *Evaluating the Arts in Education: A Responsive Approach.* Columbus, Ohio: Merrill, 1975.

Tufte, E. R. *Visual Explanations: Images and Quantities, Evidence and Narrative.* Cheshire, Conn.: Graphics Press, 1997.

U.S. General Accounting Office. *Record Linkage and Privacy.* Washington, D.C.: U.S. General Accounting Office, forthcoming.

Watt, J. H. "Internet Systems for Evaluation Research." In G. Gay and T. L. Bennington (eds.), *Information Technologies in Evaluation: Social, Moral, Epistemological, and Practical Implications.* New Directions for Evaluation, no. 84. San Francisco: Jossey-Bass, 1999.

Weiss, C. H. "The Stakeholder Approach to Evaluation: Origins and Promise." In A. S. Byrk (ed.), *Stakeholder-Based Evaluation.* New Directions for Program Evaluation, no. 17. San Francisco: Jossey-Bass, 1983.

Weiss, C. H. *Evaluation: Methods for Studying Programs and Policies.* (2nd ed.) Englewood Cliffs, N.J.: Prentice Hall, 1998.

Wholey, J. S. "Assessing the Feasibility and Likely Usefulness of Evaluation." In J. S. Wholey, H. P. Hatry, and K. E. Newcomer (eds.), *Handbook of Practical Program Evaluation.* San Francisco: Jossey-Bass, 1994.

Wildavsky, A. *Speaking Truth to Power.* New York: Little, Brown, 1979.

Yeh, S. S. "Building the Knowledge Base for Improving Educational and Social Programs Through Planned Variation Evaluations." *American Journal of Evaluation,* 2000, 21(1), 27–40.

VALERIE J. CARACELLI is senior social science analyst in the Center for Evaluation Methods and Issues at the U.S. General Accounting Office. She serves as chair for the Topical Interest Group on Evaluation Use.

INDEX

Back Issue/Subscription Order Form

Copy or detach and send to:
Jossey-Bass Inc., Publishers, 350 Sansome Street, San Francisco CA 94104-1342

Call or fax toll free!
Phone 888-378-2537 6AM-5PM PST; Fax 800-605-2665

Back issues: Please send me the following issues at $23 each.
(Important: please include series initials and issue number, such as EV77.)

1. EV _____

_____

_____

$ _____ Total for single issues

$ _____ Shipping charges (for single issues *only;* subscriptions are exempt from shipping charges): Up to $30, add $5^{50} • $30^{01}–$50, add $6^{50} $50^{01}–$75, add $7^{50} • $75^{01}–$100, add $9 • $100^{01}–$150, add $10 Over $150, call for shipping charge.

Subscriptions Please ❑ start ❑ renew my subscription to *New Directions for Evaluation* for the year ____ at the following rate:

❑ Individual $65 ❑ Institutional $118
NOTE: Subscriptions are quarterly, and are for the calendar year only. Subscriptions begin with the spring issue of the year indicated above. For shipping outside the U.S., please add $25.

$ _____ Total single issues and subscriptions (CA, IN, NJ, NY and DC residents, add sales tax for single issues. NY and DC residents must include shipping charges when calculating sales tax. NY and Canadian residents only, add sales tax for subscriptions.)

❑ Payment enclosed (U.S. check or money order only.)

❑ VISA, MC, AmEx, Discover Card #_____ Exp. date_____

Signature _____ Day phone _____

❑ Bill me (U.S. institutional orders only. Purchase order required.)

Purchase order #_____

Name _____

Address _____

_____

_____

Phone_____ E-mail _____

For more information about Jossey-Bass Publishers, visit our Web site at:
www.josseybass.com **PRIORITY CODE = ND1**

Other Titles Available in the
New Directions for Evaluation Series
Jennifer C. Greene, Gary T. Henry, Coeditors-in-Chief